The
AQUARIUS
Path

YOUR DAILY 2026 HOROSCOPE GUIDE

AMANDA M CLARKE

Copyright © Amanda M Clarke 2025
KORU Publishing

All rights reserved. All content, materials, and intellectual property in this book or any other platform owned by Koru Publishing are protected by copyright laws. This includes text, images, graphics, videos, audio, software, and any other form of content that may be produced by Koru Publishing.

No part of this content may be reproduced, distributed, or transmitted in any form or by any means without the prior written permission of Koru Publishing. This means that you cannot copy, reproduce, or use any of the content in this book for commercial or personal purposes without the express written consent of Koru Publishing.

Unauthorized use of any copyrighted material owned by Koru Publishing may result in legal action being taken against you. Koru Publishing reserves the right to pursue all available legal remedies against any individual or entity found to be infringing on its copyright.

In summary, Koru Publishing © 2025 holds exclusive rights to all the content produced by it, and any unauthorized use of such content will result in legal action.

KORU Publishing

KORU (Maori:NZ)
A symbol of spiritual growth and spiritual connection.

Rocky Point Townhouse, CHRISTMAS ISLAND, Western Australia 6798

ISBN: 978-1-923614-01-7

Welcome to The Aquarius Path: Your Daily 2026 Horoscope Guide — your intuitive, future-focused companion for the year ahead. Crafted for the independent, visionary, and quietly unconventional Aquarius, this guide celebrates the way you move through life — with originality, curiosity, and a heart that thrives on freedom and truth.

Inside, you'll find daily horoscopes paired with affirmations designed to work in harmony with your natural strengths. Each reading is here to help you move through 2026 with intention, whether you're exploring new ideas, nurturing authentic connections, tending to your well-being, or building the future only you can imagine.

This isn't about conformity — it's about authenticity. As you turn each page, you'll gather insight, encouragement, and cosmic reminders to trust your instincts and embrace your uniqueness. Let this be the year you innovate, expand, and fully claim the magic of living in tune with both your spirit and the stars.

Disclaimer: The Aquarius Path: Your daily 2026 horoscope guide book provides information on astrological readings and intuative interpretations, it is not intended as a substitute for professional advice, diagnosis, or treatment. The information contained in this book is provided for educational and entertainment purposes only and is not meant to be taken as specific advice for individual circumstances. The author and publisher make no representations or warranties with respect to the accuracy or completeness of the contents of this book and specifically disclaim any implied warranties of merchantability or fitness for a particular purpose. The reader should always consult with a licensed professional for any specific concerns or questions. The author and publisher shall not be liable for any loss or damage caused or alleged to have been caused, directly or indirectly, by the information contained in this book. The use of this book is at the reader's sole risk

January 2026

Aquarius
01 January 2026

The year begins with a strong lunar influence urging you to review your intentions. Aquarius, you are being asked to clarify what really matters. Saturn reminds you to respect boundaries, but Uranus gives you a wild spark of rebellion. Today is about balancing discipline with freedom. Expect conversations around money, resources, or new collaborations. Take time to write your goals, but leave space for surprises. Trust that your uniqueness is your currency—don't dilute it for approval.

Affirmation & Gratitude

I honor my individuality and welcome 2026 with clarity, courage, and openness to unexpected blessings.

Aquarius
02 January 2026

The Moon forms aspects with Mercury today, sharpening your intuition and communication skills. Your words hold power, Aquarius—don't waste them. If you've been sitting on an idea, it's time to share it. Others are ready to listen, but keep your delivery grounded. Emotionally, you may feel pulled between retreat and social engagement. Choose selectively. A friend may bring sudden insight or opportunity, so stay receptive. Use today to network wisely, while ensuring you honor your inner rhythm.

Affirmation & Gratitude

I trust my voice and share my ideas with confidence, attracting the right people and opportunities with ease.

Aquarius
03 January 2026

Relationships take the spotlight today as Venus influences your chart. Someone may seek your guidance or support, and your humanitarian nature shines. However, avoid overextending yourself to fix others' problems. Balance giving with maintaining your emotional reserves. Creative energy is strong—channel it into art, writing, or brainstorming. Love is expressed through thoughtful actions, not grand gestures. If you're single, you may sense a new romantic energy stirring. Stay open without losing your independence.

Affirmation & Gratitude

I nurture meaningful connections while honoring my own needs, allowing love and creativity to flow in balanced harmony.

Aquarius
04 January 2026

Today may feel like a push-and-pull between work obligations and personal dreams. Mars fuels your ambition, yet Neptune whispers of rest. Aquarius, you can do both—take action on tasks while giving yourself permission to daydream and envision. Practical steps aligned with a bigger vision bring success. Avoid unnecessary arguments with authority figures; choose diplomacy. Your unique approach will stand out at work if you stay true to your perspective.

Affirmation & Gratitude

I balance action with imagination, staying grounded while allowing my dreams to inspire purposeful steps forward.

Aquarius
05 January 2026

The energy shifts toward your finances and security. Aquarius, review your spending and investments—2026 wants you to take ownership of your material world. Don't fear restructuring or making bold choices if it means creating long-term stability. A conversation about shared resources could arise; transparency is key. Emotional triggers may surface around money but see them as signals to grow wiser. Abundance is not just money—it's also time, health, and energy.

Affirmation & Gratitude

I embrace abundance in all forms, making smart choices that honor my worth and future security.

Aquarius
06 January 2026

You may feel restless today as Uranus stirs your adventurous side. Travel, study, or spiritual exploration calls to you. Break routine in small ways if you can't take big leaps yet. Intellectual stimulation is crucial now—seek a book, podcast, or mentor that sparks your curiosity. An unexpected conversation could shift your worldview. Don't dismiss it, Aquarius; synchronicities are guiding you toward growth. Follow inspiration, even if it feels unconventional.

Affirmation & Gratitude

I welcome new perspectives and adventures, trusting every experience expands my wisdom and lights the path ahead.

Aquarius
07 January 2026

A powerful day for self-expression. The Moon in your sign highlights your individuality, making you magnetic. People notice your authenticity, so don't hide it. This is an excellent time to set intentions around identity and personal growth. Be mindful of impatience—it's easy to clash with others if you push too hard. Instead, channel energy into projects or activities that excite you. Aquarius, today you're being asked to fully claim your unique place in the world.

Affirmation & Gratitude

I stand in my authentic power, radiating confidence and attracting opportunities aligned with my highest self.

Aquarius
08 January 2026

The energy today is all about grounding your plans. Saturn, your co-ruler, whispers of responsibility, while Jupiter expands your sense of possibility. Aquarius, you may feel torn between what feels safe and what feels adventurous. The truth is you need both. Conversations around career direction or life structure could arise, bringing clarity if you listen without defensiveness. Practical actions will move you forward, but don't neglect your need for inspiration. Allow yourself to dream while keeping one foot steady on the ground. Progress comes from balancing discipline with hope.

Affirmation & Gratitude

I ground my dreams in steady action, trusting each step builds the foundation for my greater vision.

Aquarius
09 January 2026

Today highlights your connections and networks. The Moon lights up your friendship sector, encouraging collaborations and new alliances. Pay attention to who shows up now—these people may play important roles later in the year. Social settings bring insights and laughter, but avoid draining group dynamics. You don't need to please everyone, Aquarius. Focus on quality, not quantity. You may also receive unexpected news from a friend that sparks your creativity. Trust that community is a key part of your growth in 2026.

Affirmation & Gratitude

I attract supportive connections that uplift and inspire me, valuing quality relationships over empty crowds.

Aquarius
10 January 2026

Rest and introspection take priority today. The cosmic energy urges you to retreat inward, Aquarius, even if the world demands otherwise. This is a powerful day for meditation, journaling, or creative expression in private. Old emotions may resurface—don't run from them, observe them. Healing happens when you give yourself space to feel. You're recharging for the next cycle, so don't push productivity. Instead, honor your need for quiet and solitude. Listen closely to dreams and intuitive nudges—they hold guidance for your next steps.

Affirmation & Gratitude

I honor my inner world, allowing rest, reflection, and intuition to guide my renewal and healing.

Aquarius
11 January 2026

A fresh wave of energy arrives today, pulling you out of retreat mode. With the Moon entering your sign, Aquarius, you feel renewed. This is an excellent day to start something new, especially personal projects or wellness goals. You may feel extra sensitive to others' reactions, but don't let that sway you. Trust your instincts. Self-expression is favored—dress boldly, speak honestly, or share your creative ideas. Your individuality is magnetic today, and people notice when you step fully into your truth.

Affirmation & Gratitude

I shine authentically, embracing my uniqueness as a source of strength, joy, and opportunity.

Aquarius
12 January 2026

Conversations around values, self-worth, or finances are highlighted today. Mercury's alignment suggests a practical breakthrough in how you think about money or resources. It may be time to shift from scarcity thinking into an abundance mindset. Look for opportunities to reorganize or streamline your budget without fear. A mentor or peer may share advice that changes your perspective. Aquarius, your worth is not just measured in material success but in the richness of your contributions. Today asks you to see abundance differently.

Affirmation & Gratitude

I embrace my worth fully, knowing abundance flows to me through many channels beyond money.

Aquarius
13 January 2026

Dynamic energy fills the day, with Mars encouraging decisive action. Aquarius, it's time to take a bold step toward a long-delayed plan. Don't let self-doubt or hesitation stop you—courage is rewarded now. Others may resist your ideas at first, but persistence pays off. Channel restlessness into physical activity or creative projects to avoid frustration. This is a day where confidence brings breakthroughs. Remember, your originality is your strength—lean into it without apology.

Affirmation & Gratitude

I act with courage and conviction, knowing every bold step aligns me closer to my vision.

Aquarius
14 January 2026

Relationships come into sharper focus today. Venus encourages deeper bonds but also tests where imbalance exists. Aquarius, if you've been giving more than receiving, this is your cue to adjust. Don't shy away from honest conversations—diplomacy and truth can coexist. This energy favors partnerships, whether romantic or professional, especially if they allow you to remain independent within the connection. Seek relationships that nurture your individuality rather than restrict it. Balance and harmony are the themes.

Affirmation & Gratitude

I value balanced relationships, giving and receiving love with honesty, trust, and respect.

Aquarius
15 January 2026

The energy today brings a deep dive into your subconscious. Aquarius, hidden emotions or past patterns may surface, offering you clarity. Don't shy away from this inner work—what comes up now is ready to be released. Pay attention to dreams, intuitive flashes, or recurring thoughts. They're not random; they are guiding you toward healing. Instead of avoiding discomfort, lean into it with curiosity. Journaling, meditation, or quiet reflection will help unlock answers you've been seeking. The universe is clearing space for your next chapter.

Affirmation & Gratitude

I embrace inner healing, releasing old patterns and welcoming clarity, peace, and freedom into my life.

Aquarius
16 January 2026

Energy shifts toward self-empowerment today. The Moon connects with Mars, fueling your drive and determination. Aquarius, you may feel ready to finally tackle a project or conversation you've avoided. Confidence comes naturally now, but remember to balance assertiveness with patience. Others may not move as quickly as you, and that's okay. This is an excellent day to stand in your truth and advocate for yourself. Even small steps today set powerful change in motion.

Affirmation & Gratitude

I stand confidently in my truth, taking empowered steps toward my goals with courage and grace.

Aquarius
17 January 2026

Community and social connections take center stage. Aquarius, you may be invited to join an event, gathering, or collaborative project. Say yes if it excites you, but don't overcommit. Your energy is magnetic, drawing new allies who support your growth. Pay attention to conversations—someone may spark an idea that evolves into something bigger down the line. The cosmos highlights your role as a connector, but remember, your time and energy are valuable. Share them wisely.

Affirmation & Gratitude

I welcome uplifting connections, embracing collaboration while honoring my boundaries and energy.

Aquarius
18 January 2026

A slower pace calls today. Aquarius, you may feel like retreating from the noise of life. This is an ideal day to rest, recharge, or engage in spiritual practices. Don't feel guilty for stepping back—solitude is essential for your creativity and emotional balance. Insights come when you quiet your mind. If restlessness arises, channel it into journaling or creative expression. This pause allows you to reconnect with your deeper self, strengthening your clarity for what's ahead.

Affirmation & Gratitude
I honor rest and solitude, allowing stillness to nourish my spirit and inspire fresh clarity.

Aquarius
19 January 2026

The Sun enters Aquarius today—your season officially begins! Energy shifts in your favor, highlighting your individuality, confidence, and personal goals. This is the perfect moment to set intentions for the year ahead. You'll feel renewed vitality and magnetism, making it easier to attract opportunities and support. Aquarius, step boldly into the spotlight without fear of judgment. Your uniqueness is your strength, and now the world is ready to see it. Celebrate your season by honoring your true self.

Affirmation & Gratitude

I celebrate my season, embracing my authentic self and shining brightly with confidence, joy, and purpose.

Aquarius
20 January 2026

Fresh ideas flow today as Mercury energizes your sign, sharpening your intellect and curiosity. Aquarius, your mind is racing with possibilities—capture them before they slip away. This is a powerful day for brainstorming, planning, and sharing innovative ideas. Others are receptive to your insights, so don't hold back. Be mindful not to scatter your focus across too many projects. Pick one or two and commit. Conversations with like-minded people could spark collaborations that shape your year ahead.

Affirmation & Gratitude

I welcome fresh ideas and share my insights with clarity, attracting opportunities that align with my vision

Aquarius
21 January 2026

Today's energy highlights relationships and partnerships. Aquarius, you may feel the need to evaluate how balanced your closest bonds are. Are you giving more than you're receiving, or are you holding back out of fear of vulnerability? Venus encourages honesty, but diplomacy will keep conversations smooth. This is a good day for building bridges or resolving tension, especially if you've avoided addressing something. Don't sacrifice your independence, but allow yourself to lean into genuine connection. Partnerships thrive when freedom and respect walk hand in hand.

Affirmation & Gratitude

I welcome balanced partnerships, embracing love and respect while honoring my independence and truth.

Aquarius
22 January 2026

The Moon activates your career sector, pushing you to focus on ambitions and public image. Aquarius, today's efforts can bring recognition if you're consistent and professional. Opportunities for leadership may arise, but avoid being overly rebellious with authority figures—save innovation for where it's welcomed. Your ideas shine brighter when grounded in practicality. This is also a good day to review long-term goals and adjust your path if needed. Remember, progress is built step by step, not overnight.

Affirmation & Gratitude

I take steady steps toward success, aligning ambition with integrity and purpose.

Aquarius
23 January 2026

Restless energy surfaces today, urging you to break free from routine. Aquarius, you thrive on innovation, so introduce fresh elements into your day. Try a new route, shift your schedule, or explore an interest that excites you. The universe is nudging you to step out of autopilot and engage with life differently. Be cautious with impulsive decisions, though—freedom feels good but avoid unnecessary chaos. Inspiration flows when you allow yourself small experiments without fear of failure.

Affirmation & Gratitude

I embrace change with curiosity, trusting new experiences to expand my growth and joy.

Aquarius
24 January 2026

Emotional depth takes over as the Moon enters your introspective zone. Aquarius, you may crave solitude or time with a trusted confidant. Old wounds may resurface, but today offers a chance for deep healing. Don't suppress emotions—let them flow and release. Meditation or journaling will bring clarity, while creative outlets can help process feelings. By evening, you'll feel lighter, as if you've shed unnecessary baggage. Remember, vulnerability is not weakness—it's part of your strength.

Affirmation & Gratitude

I allow healing to flow through me, releasing old pain and embracing renewal.

Aquarius
25 January 2026

A burst of energy brings a desire to act boldly. Mars influences your sign today, sparking courage and initiative. Aquarius, you may feel impatient, but channel that fire into constructive action. Start a project, share your ideas, or take a physical challenge. Just avoid unnecessary conflict—people may not keep pace with you. Leadership opportunities could present themselves, and your forward-thinking approach will be appreciated if you stay respectful. Today is about courage, not recklessness.

Affirmation & Gratitude
I act with courage and purpose, channeling my energy into meaningful, positive action.

Aquarius
26 January 2026

Your friendships and networks are in focus again. Aquarius, social invitations or group collaborations may appear, giving you chances to expand your influence. This is an excellent time to reconnect with allies who inspire you or to step into a new community aligned with your goals. Avoid spreading yourself thin—choose gatherings that energize rather than drain. A group conversation may spark a new vision for the future, so pay attention to synchronicities.

Affirmation & Gratitude

I attract uplifting communities, surrounding myself with people who share vision, laughter, and support.

Aquarius
27 January 2026

The cosmos urges balance today. You may feel pulled between responsibilities and personal desires. Aquarius, multitasking is tempting, but it could scatter your focus. Instead, prioritize with intention. Don't be afraid to delegate or say no if needed—protecting your energy is essential. This is also a day for practical self-care—organize your schedule, tidy your space, and nourish your body. Small acts of structure will bring peace of mind and clarity.

Affirmation & Gratitude

I create balance by honoring priorities, protecting my energy, and choosing actions that serve my well-being.

Aquarius
28 January 2026

Today emphasizes creativity and self-expression. Aquarius, your ideas are innovative, and people are ready to listen. Whether through art, writing, speaking, or problem-solving, your originality stands out. Don't dismiss your ideas as "too different"—that's exactly what makes them powerful. Share them boldly, even if only with a small group. Romance is also highlighted, with playful energy encouraging connection through humor and lightness. Avoid self-criticism—perfection isn't required, only authenticity. Let joy fuel your expression.

Affirmation & Gratitude

I express myself freely, celebrating my creativity and uniqueness without apology.

Aquarius
29 January 2026

The Moon highlights your home and family zone today. You may feel pulled toward domestic matters—organizing, beautifying, or addressing emotional ties with loved ones. Aquarius, don't neglect your roots while chasing the future. Sometimes grounding yourself in your environment restores clarity and balance. If tension arises with family, respond with patience. Healing comes from understanding, not winning an argument. Nurture your space with love and create a sanctuary that reflects your spirit.

Affirmation & Gratitude

I create peace in my home, nurturing harmony and love within my sacred space.

Aquarius
30 January 2026

Energy surges in your career and ambition sector today. Aquarius, this is a day to step into leadership or showcase your expertise. Don't shy away from visibility—your innovative ideas need a platform. A breakthrough may arrive through recognition from others, but don't rely solely on external approval. Ground your achievements with integrity. Avoid clashes with authority figures by keeping your focus professional and results-driven. Bold action now sets the tone for future progress.

Affirmation & Gratitude
I rise with confidence, sharing my talents and embracing success with humility and strength.

Aquarius
31 January 2026

The month ends with a reflective note. Aquarius, today encourages you to slow down, evaluate January's lessons, and prepare for February's fresh energy. Celebrate your progress, no matter how small. Look at where you've grown, released old patterns, or taken bold steps. The universe asks you to acknowledge your resilience and uniqueness. This is not a day for heavy lifting but for gratitude, reflection, and gentle preparation. Rest now will fuel the month ahead.

Affirmation & Gratitude

I reflect with gratitude, honoring my growth and preparing for the opportunities February brings.

February 2026

Aquarius
01 February 2026

February begins with a burst of forward-thinking energy. Aquarius, the cosmos highlights your innovative streak, making this an excellent day for brainstorming and starting new ventures. Others may finally see the brilliance of an idea you've been carrying quietly. Don't hesitate to share it—your originality inspires. Be mindful of restlessness; grounding rituals like walking in nature or mindful breathing will steady your pace. Balance freedom with structure, and you'll discover momentum that lasts beyond today.

Affirmation & Gratitude

I step into February with clarity and courage, embracing my originality as a guiding force for success.

Aquarius
02 February 2026

Today's energy highlights finances and values. Aquarius, review your relationship with money—are you investing wisely or holding onto fears of lack? The universe asks you to redefine abundance. Opportunities may come through a conversation or unexpected insight. Think long-term security, not just quick wins. Emotional triggers around self-worth may surface, reminding you that your value extends beyond numbers in a bank account. Use today to make empowered choices that honor both your resources and your spirit.

Affirmation & Gratitude

I value myself fully, attracting abundance that aligns with my worth and long-term vision.

Aquarius
03 February 2026

Communication flows easily today as Mercury enhances your words and ideas. Aquarius, you have the gift of explaining complex topics in simple ways, making others eager to listen. This is an ideal day for meetings, writing, teaching, or sharing knowledge. Pay attention to synchronicities in conversations—someone may drop a clue that sparks inspiration. Keep your mind open, and don't rush; clarity comes from listening as much as speaking. Journal your insights, as they may become important later.

Affirmation & Gratitude

I speak with clarity and listen with wisdom, trusting my words and ideas reach the right hearts.

Aquarius
04 February 2026

Home and inner sanctuary come into focus today. Aquarius, you may crave coziness, solitude, or quality time with loved ones. Use this energy to create harmony in your environment. Clean, reorganize, or add something beautiful to your space—it will refresh your spirit. Emotional matters within family may need attention; listen with compassion rather than reacting. Nurturing your foundations allows you to feel supported as you move forward with bigger goals.

Affirmation & Gratitude
I create peace within my home, nurturing my sanctuary with love, patience, and gratitude.

Aquarius
05 February 2026

A fiery wave of ambition sparks today. Aquarius, Mars energizes your career zone, urging bold moves. Whether it's pitching an idea, stepping into leadership, or simply showing your skills, courage brings recognition. Others may challenge your ideas, but don't shrink back—stay firm while remaining respectful. Channel restlessness into action that supports long-term goals. This is not a day for hesitation but for trusting your capabilities. Your innovative edge is your advantage.

Affirmation & Gratitude

I act with courage and determination, trusting my talents to open doors of opportunity.

Aquarius
06 February 2026

Relationships feel lighter and more joyful today. Aquarius, Venus blesses your chart with harmony, making it easier to connect with others. Romance is highlighted—whether deepening a bond or sparking something new, today is about celebrating love in all forms. Friendships also bring laughter and support. Remember to receive as well as give; allow others to show up for you. Shared experiences will leave you feeling uplifted and recharged.

Affirmation & Gratitude

I welcome love and joy into my connections, embracing harmony and laughter with an open heart.

Aquarius
07 February 2026

Intuition is strong today, Aquarius. You may receive flashes of insight, gut feelings, or vivid dreams that guide you toward clarity. Don't ignore them—write them down or act on small nudges. Today is ideal for spiritual practices, meditation, or creative flow that feels divinely inspired. Avoid overanalyzing; not everything needs logic. Trust the invisible threads guiding you forward. If you quiet the noise, the answers you seek are already within you.

Affirmation & Gratitude

I trust my intuition, allowing inner wisdom to guide me toward truth and alignment.

Aquarius
08 February 2026

The energy today invites you to slow down and reflect. Aquarius, after a socially active period, your spirit craves solitude. Use this time to check in with yourself—how are your goals aligning with your inner truth? Avoid overcommitting; rest and silence will bring clarity. Emotional memories may arise, but they carry lessons rather than burdens. Release what no longer supports your growth. Journaling, meditation, or even a long walk outdoors will help you reconnect with your essence.

Affirmation & Gratitude

I honor my need for stillness, knowing rest and reflection strengthen my path forward.

Aquarius
09 February 2026

Today the Moon highlights your sign, boosting your magnetism and self-expression. Aquarius, you feel more seen and recognized, which encourages you to take bold steps. This is the perfect day to start a personal project, launch an idea, or showcase your creativity. Be mindful of impatience—others may not keep pace with your visionary thinking. Trust that those who need your spark will notice. The universe encourages you to embrace visibility and authenticity without hesitation.

Affirmation & Gratitude

I shine authentically, sharing my truth and creativity with confidence and joy.

Aquarius
10 February 2026

Practical matters demand attention today. Aquarius, the cosmic energy emphasizes finances, work tasks, and organization. While your mind may wander to visionary plans, grounding yourself in detail-oriented work will pay off. Review budgets, contracts, or long-term commitments. This is not the day for shortcuts—precision and patience will strengthen your foundation. By handling practicalities now, you create space for freedom later. Avoid overspending, as emotional purchases may tempt you. Choose discipline instead.

Affirmation & Gratitude

I strengthen my foundation through wise choices, knowing each step builds long-term freedom.

Aquarius
11 February 2026

Conversations and ideas take the spotlight. Aquarius, your mind is sharp and curious, making this a great day for learning, networking, or sharing your insights. Social energy feels lively, and you may connect with someone who broadens your perspective. Be open to unexpected opportunities that come through casual exchanges. If restlessness arises, channel it into writing or creative expression. Remember, your ideas are seeds—nurture them with consistency. Don't scatter your focus.

Affirmation & Gratitude

I welcome conversations that inspire growth, valuing every exchange as a doorway to opportunity.

Aquarius
12 February 2026

Emotions run deep today as the Moon lights up your family and roots sector. Aquarius, you may feel nostalgic or drawn to reflect on your past. Healing energy surrounds relationships with parents or close relatives. If tension surfaces, seek understanding rather than defense. This is also a good day for creating comfort in your home—tidying, decorating, or simply enjoying quiet time. Your stability grows when your personal sanctuary feels aligned and nurturing.

Affirmation & Gratitude

I create harmony within my home and family, allowing love and understanding to guide my actions.

Aquarius
13 February 2026

A surge of ambition arrives, Aquarius. You may feel motivated to pursue career opportunities or assert yourself in leadership roles. Today is about visibility—others are watching, and your originality makes you stand out. Avoid defensiveness with authority figures; diplomacy paired with confidence wins. If you've been hesitating to showcase a project, now is the time to step up. Bold yet measured action propels you forward. Remember, success is not luck—it's alignment and effort.

Affirmation & Gratitude

I step confidently into leadership, trusting my talents to open the right doors.

Aquarius
14 February 2026

Valentine's Day carries sweet energy this year, Aquarius. Venus highlights love and connection, bringing harmony to relationships. Whether partnered or single, today reminds you of the joy in celebrating love in all forms—romantic, platonic, and self-love. Laughter, creativity, and warmth are your guiding lights. Avoid getting caught up in expectations; focus instead on presence and sincerity. A small gesture may have greater meaning than a grand display. Your heart opens widest when you embrace authenticity.

Affirmation & Gratitude

I celebrate love in all forms, sharing joy and kindness with openness and gratitude.

Aquarius
15 February 2026

Today highlights balance between work and personal life. Aquarius, you may feel stretched between responsibilities and your desire for freedom. The cosmos asks you to prioritize without guilt—delegate where possible, and don't overpromise. Your well-being depends on setting healthy boundaries. At work, productivity thrives if you stay organized, but avoid burning out by saying yes to everything. In personal life, carve out moments of joy to restore balance. Remember, success feels hollow if your spirit is neglected.

Affirmation & Gratitude

I create balance by honoring my responsibilities while protecting time for joy and self-care.

Aquarius
16 February 2026

Energy today favors deep thinking and problem-solving. Aquarius, your mind is sharp, intuitive, and ready to uncover hidden truths. Pay attention to details, because small observations may reveal big insights. If you've been puzzling over a decision, clarity begins to form now. Don't be afraid to explore unconventional approaches—they may be exactly what's needed. This is also a good day for research or learning. Trust that curiosity leads to growth and surprising discoveries.

Affirmation & Gratitude

I welcome insight and clarity, trusting curiosity to guide me toward truth and understanding.

Aquarius
17 February 2026

Relationships come into focus under today's energy. Aquarius, conversations with loved ones or partners may bring important realizations. If something has felt unbalanced, now is the time to discuss it openly. Approach with honesty but also compassion. This is also a favorable day for collaboration—working with others will spark fresh ideas. The lesson is to embrace interdependence without losing independence. Balance and respect are key themes today.

Affirmation & Gratitude

I honor honesty and compassion in relationships, welcoming harmony and shared understanding.

Aquarius
18 February 2026

The Sun moves into Pisces, shifting the energy toward finances, values, and self-worth. Aquarius, over the coming weeks you'll be encouraged to focus on stability and abundance. Today, you may feel called to reassess budgets or clarify what truly matters to you. Value is not only material—it's also time, energy, and personal fulfillment. Begin aligning your actions with your deeper priorities, and abundance will follow.

Affirmation & Gratitude
I align with what I value most, creating abundance through mindful choices.

Aquarius
19 February 2026

Creative sparks fly today. Aquarius, your imagination is active, making this an excellent day for art, writing, or innovative projects. Don't dismiss unusual ideas—they may hold the key to breakthroughs. Playfulness and joy are also emphasized, so allow yourself time to relax and have fun. Romance may feel lighthearted and exciting, adding sweetness to your day. Express yourself authentically without worrying about judgment; the right people will celebrate your originality.

Affirmation & Gratitude

I express my creativity with joy, trusting my originality to inspire and uplift.

Aquarius
20 February 2026

Reflection takes center stage as emotions run deeper. Aquarius, you may crave solitude to process inner feelings. Old wounds or memories may resurface, but they bring healing if acknowledged. Instead of pushing discomfort aside, listen to what it teaches you. This is a powerful day for meditation, journaling, or releasing rituals. Growth often comes quietly, in moments of honesty with yourself. Don't underestimate the strength in stillness.

Affirmation & Gratitude
I honor my inner world, finding healing and wisdom in quiet reflection.

Aquarius
21 February 2026

The cosmos pushes you into the spotlight again, Aquarius. Opportunities for recognition or leadership may arise, particularly in professional spaces. Your innovative ideas are seen as valuable—don't downplay them. Confidence is your ally, but temper it with diplomacy to avoid friction with authority figures. This is a day to act boldly, showcasing your abilities without fear of rejection. Trust that authenticity wins respect and opens doors.

Affirmation & Gratitude

I step into the spotlight with confidence, sharing my gifts boldly and authentically.

Aquarius
22 February 2026

Today emphasizes friendships and community. Aquarius, your role as a connector is highlighted, making this a perfect day to collaborate or engage socially. You may meet someone who introduces fresh opportunities, or an existing friend could offer support. Be mindful not to scatter your energy across too many groups—focus on meaningful connections. Collective energy inspires you, but don't lose your individuality in the crowd. Your ideas spark inspiration, so don't hesitate to share them.

Affirmation & Gratitude

I attract uplifting connections, embracing friendships that encourage growth, laughter, and shared vision.

Aquarius
23 February 2026

Rest and solitude are calling. Aquarius, you've been highly social, and now your spirit craves quiet. Use today to recharge physically and emotionally. A retreat into stillness will sharpen your intuition, helping you process recent events. Dreams or meditations may bring unexpected guidance. Don't push productivity; instead, allow space for reflection. By evening, you'll feel more centered and ready to move forward. Remember, pausing is not weakness—it's wisdom.

Affirmation & Gratitude

I restore my energy in solitude, honoring the wisdom that comes from silence.

Aquarius
24 February 2026

The Moon moves into your sign, giving you a burst of confidence and presence. Aquarius, today you're magnetic, and others notice your authenticity. This is an ideal time to set intentions around personal growth and identity. Don't shy away from visibility—share your talents and ideas without fear. You may feel restless, but channel this energy into creative expression or self-care that strengthens your confidence. Your individuality is your greatest gift.

Affirmation & Gratitude

I embrace my uniqueness, stepping into the world with confidence and joy.

Aquarius
25 February 2026

Finances and resources are highlighted today. Aquarius, review your spending, savings, and long-term plans. A practical conversation may arise about money, possessions, or security. Don't avoid it—clarity will empower you. Avoid impulsive purchases, as restlessness could tempt you to spend unnecessarily. Instead, think about what truly adds value to your life. Building stability now will bring freedom later. Abundance flows when you align your actions with your values.

Affirmation & Gratitude

I make wise choices with my resources, creating stability that supports freedom and growth.

Aquarius
26 February 2026

Communication flows smoothly today. Aquarius, Mercury enhances your ability to share ideas and connect meaningfully. Expect lively conversations, new insights, or even surprising news. This is a great day for writing, networking, or presenting your vision. Be mindful not to scatter your energy —focus on one or two key priorities. People are listening, so choose words that uplift and inspire. Your originality makes your message unforgettable.

Affirmation & Gratitude

I communicate clearly and authentically, trusting my words to reach the right ears.

Aquarius
27 February 2026

Emotional matters at home or within family may need attention. Aquarius, the cosmos highlights your roots, urging you to nurture your foundation. Whether it's resolving tension, spending time with loved ones, or making your living space more harmonious, today calls for grounding. Don't overlook your emotional needs while chasing future goals. Stability begins within your personal sanctuary. A peaceful home supports everything else you aim to achieve.

Affirmation & Gratitude

I nurture harmony within my home and family, creating peace at my foundation.

Aquarius
28 February 2026

Ambition surges as cosmic energy lights up your career sector. Aquarius, today's efforts may bring recognition or progress in professional matters. You're seen as capable and innovative, so step into leadership if opportunities arise. Avoid clashes with authority by staying diplomatic and focusing on results. Your originality shines brightest when paired with consistency. Take bold but calculated action toward long-term success.

Affirmation & Gratitude
I embrace ambition with integrity, taking bold steps toward lasting achievement.

March
2026

Aquarius
01 March 2026

The new month begins with a spotlight on your finances and values, Aquarius. The cosmos urges you to examine where your resources are going and whether they truly serve your bigger picture. Security and freedom are not opposites—they complement one another when you make choices aligned with your deeper vision. Today, set aside time to review budgets, reflect on investments, or simply get clear about how you're spending your energy. Remember, time, health, and focus are also forms of wealth. Choose wisely, and long-term stability will follow.

Affirmation & Gratitude

I align my resources with purpose, building stability that supports freedom, growth, and peace of mind.

Aquarius
02 March 2026

Communication flows easily under today's skies. Mercury highlights your ability to share ideas with clarity, making this an excellent day for writing, speaking, or negotiating. Aquarius, your originality shines through your words, and others are ready to listen. A conversation may bring surprising insight or open a new door, so stay alert. Be mindful not to overwhelm with too much detail—keep your message simple and powerful. The universe favors connections that expand your vision. Capture any flashes of inspiration that come your way.

Affirmation & Gratitude

I share my truth clearly, trusting my words to inspire, connect, and open doors of opportunity.

Aquarius
03 March 2026

Your attention turns inward toward home and family. Aquarius, the cosmos encourages you to focus on your foundations—whether that's resolving emotional matters or improving your living environment. Today is about creating stability and comfort in your private world. A family conversation may bring healing if handled with patience. If emotions surface, allow them to teach you rather than overwhelm you. By tending to your roots, you strengthen your ability to grow outwardly. Ground yourself in rituals that bring peace and harmony.

Affirmation & Gratitude

I nurture my roots with love, creating a stable foundation that supports my future growth.

Aquarius
04 March 2026

Ambition rises as cosmic energy highlights your career zone. Aquarius, you may be recognized for your contributions or feel a push to step into leadership. This is not the time to hide your brilliance—share your innovative ideas with confidence. However, avoid unnecessary conflict with authority figures; diplomacy wins greater rewards. Progress today comes through a mix of boldness and strategy. Take one step that aligns with your long-term goals, even if it feels small. Recognition will follow consistent effort.

Affirmation & Gratitude

I step forward with courage, sharing my talents and vision with confidence and grace.

Aquarius
05 March 2026

Uranus stirs your adventurous side today, urging you to break away from routines. Aquarius, exploration brings fresh energy, whether through travel, study, or simply trying something new in your daily rhythm. Inspiration is everywhere if you stay curious. Conversations may challenge your current perspective, pushing you to expand your worldview. Don't resist change; lean into it as an opportunity for growth. Even small shifts today will spark bigger momentum later. Allow spontaneity to refresh your spirit.

Affirmation & Gratitude

I embrace new experiences with curiosity, knowing every step outside routine brings growth and expansion.

Aquarius
06 March 2026

Relationships come into focus as Venus influences your chart. Aquarius, love and connection feel highlighted today, but so does the need for balance. If you've been giving more than receiving, this is your cue to address it. Romantic sparks may appear, or an existing bond can deepen through honest conversation. Partnerships thrive when you allow yourself to be both independent and connected. Nurture bonds that support your individuality rather than restrict it. Harmony comes through mutual respect.

Affirmation & Gratitude

I welcome love and harmony, nurturing connections that support freedom, balance, and joy.

Aquarius
07 March 2026

The cosmos invites you to slow down and reflect, Aquarius. Today is best used for rest, solitude, and spiritual practices. You've been busy balancing ambition, relationships, and new experiences—now your spirit craves quiet to process and recharge. Meditation, journaling, or simply spending time in nature will restore clarity. Don't push productivity; instead, allow yourself space to reconnect with your intuition. Dreams may carry symbolic messages, so pay attention. Renewal comes when you honor stillness.

Affirmation & Gratitude

I honor stillness, allowing rest and reflection to renew my mind, body, and spirit.

Aquarius
08 March 2026

A social spark lights up your chart today, Aquarius. Friendships, group activities, and community ties feel energizing. You may be invited to collaborate on a project or reconnect with like-minded people who inspire you. Pay attention to who enters your circle now—these connections may hold long-term significance. Don't scatter your energy across too many groups; focus on quality over quantity. Networking today brings opportunities, but remember to guard your boundaries. Give where it feels natural, not where it drains you.

Affirmation & Gratitude

I attract uplifting friendships and collaborations that support my growth, vision, and joy.

Aquarius
09 March 2026

The cosmos turns your focus inward, Aquarius. After social stimulation, you may crave solitude and self-reflection. Dreams, symbols, or subtle messages carry meaning—write them down. Today is excellent for meditation, journaling, or simply pausing from the noise. Old emotions may resurface, but rather than resisting, ask what they're teaching you. Healing happens when you allow space for feelings to move through. Don't feel guilty for slowing down; you're preparing for your next surge of energy.

Affirmation & Gratitude

I honor my need for quiet, embracing rest as a sacred part of growth and healing.

Aquarius
10 March 2026

The Moon in your sign gives you magnetic energy, Aquarius. You feel seen, and your individuality shines brighter than usual. This is an ideal day to launch personal projects, set fresh goals, or express yourself boldly. Be mindful of impatience—others may not move as quickly as you'd like. Still, your authenticity makes an impact, and people are drawn to your energy. Embrace visibility today. Your uniqueness is not a weakness—it's your greatest strength.

Affirmation & Gratitude
I celebrate my authentic self, shining boldly and inspiring others with my originality.

Aquarius
11 March 2026

Finances and values become the focus. Aquarius, the universe is asking you to review what truly sustains you. Are your resources—time, money, energy—being used wisely? This is an excellent day to budget, reorganize, or make decisions about long-term stability. Avoid emotional spending, as temptation may appear. Remember, your worth is not measured by possessions but by the integrity with which you live. Security grows when your choices align with your higher vision.

Affirmation & Gratitude

I align my resources with purpose, creating stability that supports freedom and fulfillment.

Aquarius
12 March 2026

Communication is heightened today, Aquarius. Mercury sharpens your intellect, helping you explain complex ideas with ease. This is an excellent day for teaching, presenting, or sharing your insights with others. A conversation may spark a breakthrough or inspire you to take a fresh path. Stay open to feedback but trust your inner voice. Write down flashes of inspiration—they may evolve into something significant later. Balance talking with listening to maximize today's opportunities.

Affirmation & Gratitude

I share my thoughts with clarity and confidence, attracting ideas and opportunities that inspire growth.

Aquarius
13 March 2026

Your home and family sphere is activated. Aquarius, today invites you to nurture your roots—whether through spending time with loved ones, creating harmony in your living space, or resolving long-standing issues. Emotions may surface, but approach them with compassion and patience. Your sanctuary is a reflection of your inner world. By tending to it, you strengthen your sense of safety and grounding. Create comfort where you are—it supports your dreams.

Affirmation & Gratitude

I create harmony within my home and family, building peace from the inside out.

Aquarius
14 March 2026

Ambition surges as your career sector lights up. Aquarius, opportunities for recognition or leadership may present themselves. Don't shy away—your originality sets you apart. Take a bold step toward your professional vision, even if it feels small. Authority figures may test your patience, but diplomacy will carry you further than defiance. Stay confident but strategic. This is a powerful day for planting seeds of long-term success. Your consistency matters more than instant results.

Affirmation & Gratitude

I step forward with courage, trusting my originality to lead me to lasting success.

Aquarius
15 March 2026

Today's cosmic energy highlights exploration and expansion. Aquarius, your spirit is craving freedom—whether that means travel, study, or simply broadening your perspective. Unexpected insights may come through a book, a conversation, or even a documentary that shifts your outlook. The universe is encouraging you to shake free of limitations and embrace curiosity. If you've felt restless, channel that energy into planning your next adventure. Growth often comes when you take a step into the unknown, trusting it will lead somewhere meaningful.

Affirmation & Gratitude

I embrace new horizons, allowing curiosity to guide me toward growth, wisdom, and exciting opportunities.

Aquarius
16 March 2026

Relationships take center stage today. Aquarius, Venus encourages harmony, but she also reveals where balance may be lacking. If you've been carrying more than your share, it's time to gently address it. Partnerships—romantic or professional—can deepen now through honesty and mutual respect. Avoid sacrificing your individuality for peace; true connection honors freedom and equality. Today is a reminder that love flourishes when you remain authentic while allowing space for others to be themselves.

Affirmation & Gratitude

I nurture balanced relationships, giving and receiving love with honesty, freedom, and respect.

Aquarius
17 March 2026

The cosmos pulls your attention inward, highlighting reflection and rest. Aquarius, today may feel quieter, but that's intentional—you're being given space to recharge. Old emotions or hidden patterns could surface, offering valuable lessons. Rather than rushing through them, sit with the feelings. Meditation, journaling, or creative solitude can help you process. Clarity doesn't always come in action; often it arrives in silence. By evening, you may feel lighter, having released something you no longer need to carry.

Affirmation & Gratitude

I honor rest and reflection, allowing silence to bring wisdom and renewal.

Aquarius
18 March 2026

The Moon in your sign gives you an energy boost, Aquarius. Today you're magnetic, and others notice your authenticity. Use this to launch projects, share ideas, or simply stand proudly in your truth. This is not a day for shrinking into the background. Your individuality inspires those around you, even if they don't say it out loud. Trust your instincts, take bold steps, and remember that your uniqueness is the key to unlocking doors.

Affirmation & Gratitude
I shine in my truth, embracing my uniqueness as a gift to the world.

Aquarius
19 March 2026

Finances and values move into focus. Aquarius, you're being encouraged to check in on how well your money habits align with your future dreams. Avoid quick fixes or impulsive purchases. Instead, think long-term security and meaningful investment in yourself. Abundance isn't just financial—it's also time, energy, and emotional wealth. By aligning your daily choices with your bigger vision, you create freedom down the line. Today is about planting practical seeds for future abundance.

Affirmation & Gratitude

I choose wisely with my resources, creating abundance that supports freedom and peace of mind.

Aquarius
20 March 2026

Your communication zone lights up, Aquarius. Today is excellent for discussions, sharing ideas, or making presentations. Others are especially receptive to your perspective, and you may find yourself in a position to influence or teach. Stay clear, concise, and confident in your delivery. A conversation may spark a new idea that has long-term potential, so keep notes. Inspiration is everywhere if you're open to it. Listening is just as important as speaking today.

Affirmation & Gratitude

I communicate with clarity and confidence, attracting opportunities that align with my vision.

Aquarius
21 March 2026

Emotional matters tied to home or family may arise. Aquarius, the cosmos is asking you to strengthen your foundations, whether that's resolving long-standing issues or creating harmony in your living space. Your sanctuary is a reflection of your inner world—when it's peaceful, you thrive. Spend time with loved ones, nurture your environment, or release emotional baggage that has lingered. Today is about grounding yourself in what feels safe and secure, giving you strength for what's ahead.

Affirmation & Gratitude

I create harmony in my home and heart, nurturing peace at my foundation.

Aquarius
22 March 2026

Ambition rises as the cosmos lights up your career sector. Aquarius, you may feel called to step up, showcase your abilities, or pursue a bold move in your professional world. Recognition is possible today if you act with confidence. Authority figures may test your resolve, so keep diplomacy in your approach. Boldness combined with strategy ensures success. Take one practical step toward your vision, even if it feels small—momentum builds quickly now.

Affirmation & Gratitude

I act with confidence and strategy, knowing each step forward strengthens my long-term success.

Aquarius
23 March 2026

Freedom calls today as Uranus encourages exploration and breaking free of routines. Aquarius, you may crave change or adventure—follow the impulse in healthy ways. Take a different approach to a familiar problem or learn something outside your comfort zone. Conversations may challenge your perspective, pushing you to think differently. Inspiration comes when you're open to surprises. This is a day for curiosity and experimentation, not rigid plans.

Affirmation & Gratitude

I welcome change with curiosity, trusting that new experiences bring growth and fresh inspiration.

Aquarius
24 March 2026

Partnerships come into focus today. Aquarius, whether in romance, friendship, or business, relationships may bring important insights. Balance and equality are key—don't ignore areas where you're giving too much or holding back. Venus favors harmony, so honest conversations can flow more easily now. You don't have to sacrifice independence to connect deeply; true partnership embraces individuality. Seek bonds that uplift rather than restrict you. Today's energy strengthens connections built on trust.

Affirmation & Gratitude

I embrace balanced partnerships, honoring both freedom and connection in my relationships.

Aquarius
25 March 2026

Introspection calls as the Moon highlights your inner world. Aquarius, this is a quieter day best spent reflecting, journaling, or tending to your spiritual practices. Old memories or emotions may resurface, but they're here to be acknowledged and released. Don't push productivity—rest and stillness bring more clarity than action. Trust your intuition; subtle signs or dreams may reveal guidance. This is an ideal day for cleansing and renewal, both emotionally and energetically.

Affirmation & Gratitude

I honor my inner wisdom, allowing reflection to bring clarity, healing, and renewal.

Aquarius
26 March 2026

The Moon in your sign energizes you today, Aquarius. Your individuality shines, and others are drawn to your authenticity. This is an excellent time to start new projects, assert your independence, or simply enjoy being yourself without apology. You may feel impatient with others who move slower, but use this as a chance to practice patience. The universe is highlighting your uniqueness —step boldly into your truth and trust that it opens doors.

Affirmation & Gratitude

I shine authentically, embracing my uniqueness as my greatest strength.

Aquarius
27 March 2026

Finances and security take the spotlight. Aquarius, review your money habits and long-term goals. Are your current choices aligned with the stability you seek? Avoid quick fixes or emotional spending; focus instead on practical steps that build abundance over time. This energy also asks you to value your time and energy as highly as money. True wealth is balance—when you honor your resources, life flows more easily.

Affirmation & Gratitude
I make wise choices with my resources, creating stability that supports freedom and joy.

Aquarius
28 March 2026

Communication is emphasized today. Aquarius, your words carry extra influence, so use them with care. This is a great day for sharing ideas, having meaningful discussions, or learning something new. Inspiration may come through a conversation or even a chance encounter. Keep an open mind—sometimes wisdom comes from unexpected places. Balance talking with listening to get the most from today's energy. Your originality shines when you communicate authentically.

Affirmation & Gratitude

I express myself with clarity and listen with openness, trusting that every exchange brings growth.

Aquarius
29 March 2026

Emotional matters tied to home or family rise to the surface today, Aquarius. You may feel the need to nurture your private world, whether that means creating more comfort in your space, spending time with loved ones, or addressing long-standing issues. The cosmos encourages you to strengthen your foundations, for when your roots are grounded, you feel freer to grow outwardly. If conflict arises, approach with compassion rather than defensiveness. Peace at home supports peace within, giving you the stability needed to pursue your bigger visions.

Affirmation & Gratitude

I create harmony within my home and heart, nurturing peace at my foundation.

Aquarius
30 March 2026

Your ambitions are spotlighted again as career energy intensifies. Aquarius, today offers a chance to showcase your originality in professional settings or take steps toward your goals. Opportunities for recognition may appear, but they require you to step into visibility. Authority figures may test your resolve, but diplomacy and steady confidence will carry you further than defiance. This is not about rushing success —it's about planting seeds with care. Your innovative spirit attracts attention, and consistency ensures progress.

Affirmation & Gratitude

I rise with courage, sharing my talents confidently while staying grounded in integrity.

Aquarius
31 March 2026

March ends on a reflective yet visionary note. Aquarius, the cosmos invites you to pause, review the lessons of the month, and prepare for April's fresh wave of energy. What worked well? What habits or attitudes need to shift? Take time to celebrate your growth and acknowledge how far you've come. Even the smallest steps deserve recognition. Today favors journaling, meditation, or vision-setting. The universe rewards reflection, as it ensures you step forward with clarity.

Affirmation & Gratitude

I honor my growth, reflecting with gratitude and preparing with intention for what comes next.

April 2026

Aquarius
01 April 2026

April begins with a cosmic nudge toward fresh ideas and communication. Aquarius, your mind is alive with possibilities, and Mercury enhances your ability to express yourself clearly. This is an excellent day for brainstorming, writing, or reaching out to contacts who may support your goals. Be mindful not to scatter your attention too widely—choose one or two priorities to focus on. Curiosity leads to inspiration, and a conversation may provide the missing piece to a puzzle you've been trying to solve.

Affirmation & Gratitude

I welcome fresh ideas and conversations, trusting inspiration to flow where it is most needed.

Aquarius
02 April 2026

Your home and inner world come into focus today. Aquarius, you may feel pulled toward nesting, cleaning, or creating a sense of order in your personal space. The cosmos encourages you to build a sanctuary that reflects your spirit, bringing peace and grounding. Emotional matters with family may surface; if so, respond with patience and empathy. By strengthening your foundation now, you create stability that supports your larger dreams. Home is not just a place—it's your energetic base.

Affirmation & Gratitude

I create harmony and comfort within my home, grounding myself in peace and love.

Aquarius
03 April 2026

Ambition surges as cosmic energy highlights your career sector. Aquarius, today is excellent for stepping up into leadership or pushing a project forward. Recognition may come for past efforts, or new opportunities may present themselves. Avoid unnecessary clashes with authority—diplomacy will get your vision across more effectively. Take bold yet strategic steps, and remember that consistency wins long-term success. Trust that your originality is not just welcomed—it's needed. Shine confidently while staying grounded in integrity.

Affirmation & Gratitude

I step into leadership with confidence, sharing my vision boldly and authentically.

Aquarius
04 April 2026

Freedom and exploration are highlighted today. Aquarius, Uranus stirs your adventurous side, making you crave variety and new experiences. This doesn't necessarily mean a big leap—trying something different in your daily rhythm can refresh your spirit. Travel, study, or cultural activities may call to you, expanding your worldview. Don't resist change; lean into it as growth. Pay attention to unexpected insights or encounters—they may inspire your next steps. The cosmos reminds you that curiosity opens doors.

Affirmation & Gratitude
I embrace change and exploration, knowing new experiences expand my wisdom and joy.

Aquarius
05 April 2026

Partnerships take center stage, Aquarius. Venus encourages you to deepen meaningful connections, whether in romance, friendship, or business. Equality and mutual respect are emphasized—if there's imbalance, you may feel it more strongly today. Use this as an opportunity for honest conversations. True partnership doesn't restrict; it uplifts while allowing freedom. If single, you may meet someone who values your individuality. This energy supports connections built on authenticity rather than pretense.

Affirmation & Gratitude

I welcome balanced partnerships, honoring love, trust, and freedom in all my connections.

Aquarius
06 April 2026

The cosmos calls you inward today, Aquarius. Reflection, solitude, and spiritual practice bring the clarity you've been seeking. Emotions may surface, but don't suppress them—observe and release them. Dreams or intuitive nudges hold guidance, so pay attention to the subtle messages around you. This is not a day for overexertion; instead, focus on rest, journaling, or meditation. Healing comes quietly, when you give yourself permission to slow down and listen.

Affirmation & Gratitude

I honor stillness and reflection, allowing my inner wisdom to guide me.

Aquarius
07 April 2026

The Moon in your sign restores vitality, Aquarius. You feel magnetic, energized, and ready to step forward boldly. This is a great day to launch projects, make an impression, or simply embrace your individuality unapologetically. Be mindful not to become impatient with others who move slower—everyone has their rhythm. Your originality is shining brighter now, and the universe encourages you to use it confidently. Claim your space; your authenticity opens doors.

Affirmation & Gratitude

I shine in my truth, radiating confidence and embracing my individuality as a gift.

Aquarius
08 April 2026

Finances and values take the spotlight today. Aquarius, the cosmos urges you to check whether your money habits align with your long-term dreams. Avoid impulsive spending; instead, focus on building stability through thoughtful planning. Abundance is about more than money—it's also time, energy, and emotional balance. If you've been undervaluing yourself, today asks you to remember your worth. Make choices that support security while still allowing freedom. Wise decisions now will create future ease.

Affirmation & Gratitude

I honor my worth and align my resources with choices that bring freedom, stability, and peace.

Aquarius
09 April 2026

Mercury enhances your communication today, Aquarius. Words flow easily, making this an excellent time for meetings, teaching, or sharing your unique perspective. Others are receptive to your originality, so don't hesitate to speak up. A conversation could open unexpected opportunities or inspire a fresh idea. Be mindful of balance—listen as much as you talk. Inspiration may come from an unlikely source, so stay open and curious. Capture insights before they slip away.

Affirmation & Gratitude

I speak with clarity and listen with openness, welcoming inspiration from every conversation.

Aquarius
10 April 2026

Emotional matters tied to home or family may surface. Aquarius, this is a good day to nurture your private world—whether that's through spending time with loved ones, beautifying your space, or resolving old tensions. Your sanctuary is your base; when it feels peaceful, you thrive in other areas. If emotions arise, handle them gently rather than defensively. Creating balance at home gives you the grounding you need to move forward with strength.

Affirmation & Gratitude
I create harmony within my home, nurturing peace and stability at my foundation.

Aquarius
11 April 2026

Your career sector is activated today. Aquarius, opportunities for recognition or leadership could arise, but they require you to step confidently into visibility. Others are watching, and your originality is what sets you apart. Avoid clashes with authority—firm diplomacy will carry your ideas further. This is not about immediate rewards but long-term growth. Take one step toward your bigger goals, even if small. Trust that consistency now leads to success later.

Affirmation & Gratitude
I step into my career with confidence, sharing my originality and building lasting success.

Aquarius
12 April 2026

Uranus stirs your adventurous side, Aquarius. Today you may crave variety and freedom from routine. Explore new perspectives through study, travel, or simply changing your daily rhythm. Growth is sparked by curiosity and openness. Don't resist change; embrace it as part of your evolution. Conversations or encounters may challenge your worldview, helping you expand beyond limitations. Inspiration comes when you're willing to see differently. Follow the sparks that excite you today.

Affirmation & Gratitude

I welcome new experiences and perspectives, allowing curiosity to guide me toward growth and wisdom.

Aquarius
13 April 2026

Relationships are highlighted as Venus influences your chart. Aquarius, harmony is within reach, but you're also asked to check for balance. If you've been overgiving, it's time to adjust. Equality and respect create healthy partnerships, whether romantic or professional. Connection doesn't require you to give up your independence—it flourishes when both people bring their authentic selves. Today favors honesty, kindness, and meaningful connection. Choose relationships that celebrate your individuality, not diminish it.

Affirmation & Gratitude

I embrace balanced partnerships, honoring love, respect, and freedom in all my connections.

Aquarius
14 April 2026

The cosmos encourages reflection and rest. Aquarius, you've been busy juggling ambition, relationships, and new experiences—now your spirit craves quiet. Solitude, journaling, or meditation will restore clarity. Old emotions may resurface, but they're here to be acknowledged and released. Don't force productivity; today's value lies in listening to your inner world. Your intuition is strong—trust subtle nudges and symbolic dreams. Renewal happens when you slow down and honor your inner voice.

Affirmation & Gratitude

I honor stillness, allowing rest and reflection to renew my clarity and strength.

Aquarius
15 April 2026

The Moon in your sign lights you up today, Aquarius. You feel magnetic, alive, and ready to take bold steps. This is the perfect time to launch a project, set new personal intentions, or simply embrace your individuality more fully. Others notice your energy and may be inspired by your authenticity. Be mindful of impatience—everyone moves at their own pace. The universe is encouraging you to claim your space unapologetically. Step forward and let your originality shine—it's your greatest asset.

Affirmation & Gratitude

I shine authentically, stepping forward with confidence and embracing my unique gifts.

Aquarius
16 April 2026

Finances and values come into sharper focus. Aquarius, today is excellent for reviewing budgets, making long-term plans, or redefining what abundance means to you. Be mindful of unnecessary spending—impulsive choices may tempt you, but discipline will serve you better. Abundance is not just money—it's also time, energy, and peace of mind. Align your financial habits with your higher goals. The universe is reminding you that your worth is not measured in possessions but in how you honor yourself.

Affirmation & Gratitude

I align my choices with my true values, building stability that supports my freedom and dreams.

Aquarius
17 April 2026

Mercury highlights your communication sector, making this a powerful day for conversations and sharing ideas. Aquarius, your words can inspire, teach, or even change someone's perspective today. Pay attention to casual interactions—important insights may come through unexpected channels. This is also a great time to write, brainstorm, or present your ideas. Be mindful not to scatter your focus; one or two strong messages will be more impactful than ten small ones.

Affirmation & Gratitude

I communicate with clarity and confidence, trusting my words to create positive impact.

Aquarius
18 April 2026

Emotional matters around home and family may surface. Aquarius, you may feel called to create more comfort in your space or address unresolved issues. Family conversations may be healing if you approach them with compassion rather than defensiveness. Your sanctuary reflects your inner world—when your environment feels peaceful, your spirit feels supported. Use today to nurture your private life, and you'll find strength to face external challenges. Home is your anchor now.

Affirmation & Gratitude

I create peace in my home, nurturing harmony and stability at my foundation.

Aquarius
19 April 2026

Ambition and visibility rise today. Aquarius, your career zone is active, making this an ideal time to step into leadership or showcase your originality. Recognition may come for your efforts, but don't rely on external validation—stay true to your own vision. Authority figures may test your resolve, but calm confidence will serve you well. Remember, your innovation is your strength, and it's time to share it more widely.

Affirmation & Gratitude

I step into leadership with courage, trusting my originality to guide me forward.

Aquarius
20 April 2026

A surge of adventurous energy fills the day, Aquarius. Uranus encourages you to break away from routine and explore something new. Whether through travel, learning, or experimenting with fresh approaches, growth happens when you step outside your comfort zone. Don't dismiss unconventional ideas—they may hold surprising value. The universe is nudging you toward expansion, reminding you that life feels most alive when curiosity leads the way.

Affirmation & Gratitude

I embrace change and exploration, trusting curiosity to expand my life and spirit.

Aquarius
21 April 2026

Relationships are spotlighted today. Aquarius, Venus emphasizes the importance of harmony, but she also reveals where imbalance exists. Have you been giving too much or not enough? Today is about restoring equality through honest yet kind conversations. Partnerships—romantic or professional—thrive when both parties feel seen and respected. This is a reminder that love is not about sacrifice but about balance and authenticity. Nurture connections that support your individuality rather than restrict it.

Affirmation & Gratitude

I welcome balanced, respectful relationships that honor freedom and love.

Aquarius
22 April 2026

The cosmos invites you to pause and reflect, Aquarius. Today feels quieter, and that's intentional—you're being asked to recharge. Old emotions may resurface, but they're here to teach you, not overwhelm you. Give yourself space to observe without judgment. Solitude, meditation, or journaling will bring clarity. Sometimes the answers you seek come not through action, but through silence. Don't feel guilty for resting; it is part of your growth cycle. Trust the wisdom that emerges when you honor stillness.

Affirmation & Gratitude

I honor rest and reflection, trusting silence to guide me toward clarity and renewal.

Aquarius
23 April 2026

The Moon in your sign energizes you, Aquarius. You feel magnetic and ready to step into visibility. This is a great day to express yourself boldly, whether through creativity, personal style, or simply speaking your truth. Others are drawn to your authenticity, and opportunities may arrive through being unapologetically yourself. Impatience may surface, but use it as fuel to channel your energy into projects or goals that excite you. Today, the universe supports you in claiming your space.

Affirmation & Gratitude

I shine authentically, embracing my uniqueness with confidence and joy.

Aquarius
24 April 2026

Finances and values are highlighted today. Aquarius, review your spending, savings, and long-term security. Are your choices aligned with your greater goals? Emotional triggers around money may arise, but don't let them rule you—see them as guidance to make wiser decisions. This is also a good day to evaluate how you're using your time and energy. Abundance flows when you honor yourself and direct resources toward what truly matters.

Affirmation & Gratitude

I manage my resources wisely, aligning them with what brings freedom, stability, and peace.

Aquarius
25 April 2026

Conversations and ideas flow easily today. Aquarius, Mercury enhances your ability to share your perspective, making this an excellent day for writing, presenting, or networking. Your originality is inspiring, and people are drawn to your unique voice. A casual exchange may spark an important opportunity, so stay open and attentive. Remember to balance speaking with listening—insight can come from unexpected sources. Inspiration is everywhere today if you remain curious and receptive.

Affirmation & Gratitude

I communicate clearly and openly, trusting my words and ideas to reach the right people.

Aquarius
26 April 2026

Emotional matters within home and family may surface. Aquarius, today calls for patience and compassion in private matters. If tension arises, approach it with calm honesty rather than defensiveness. This is also a good day to create more harmony in your living environment—organize, decorate, or simply make your space comfortable. Your sanctuary reflects your inner world, and when it feels peaceful, you feel supported. Ground yourself in home today to restore balance and energy.

Affirmation & Gratitude
I create harmony within my home, nurturing peace and stability in my foundation.

Aquarius
27 April 2026

Your career and ambitions come to the forefront today. Aquarius, recognition may come for past efforts, or a new opportunity could present itself. Don't shy away from leadership—your originality is valued. If challenges arise with authority figures, respond with diplomacy rather than defiance. This is not about forcing progress but taking strategic steps that align with your long-term vision. Consistency now ensures sustainable growth later. The universe is encouraging you to act boldly yet wisely.

Affirmation & Gratitude

I step into leadership with courage, knowing my originality is my strength.

Aquarius
28 April 2026

Adventure and expansion are highlighted. Aquarius, Uranus stirs your curiosity, making this a day to break away from the familiar. Explore new ideas, travel, or study something that excites you. Growth comes when you stretch beyond your comfort zone. Conversations or encounters may inspire you to see the world differently, sparking a sense of renewal. This is not the time to cling to rigid plans—flow with the changes and embrace the unexpected.

Affirmation & Gratitude

I embrace new horizons with curiosity, trusting exploration to expand my wisdom and joy.

Aquarius
29 April 2026

Relationships take the spotlight today, Aquarius. Venus emphasizes connection, harmony, and balance. If you've been overextending yourself in a partnership, you may feel that imbalance more strongly now. This is the universe's reminder to restore equality. Open, honest conversations flow more smoothly today, especially when paired with kindness. For singles, this energy could bring encounters with people who resonate with your individuality. In professional settings, collaboration thrives when respect is mutual. Remember: true connection uplifts both sides, never restricts.

Affirmation & Gratitude

I nurture balanced relationships, honoring both freedom and love in all connections.

Aquarius
30 April 2026

April ends with a call for reflection and renewal. Aquarius, the cosmos encourages you to pause, review the month's lessons, and prepare for May's new momentum. Celebrate your progress, no matter how small—every step forward matters. Look at what you've learned about balance, growth, and self-worth. This is not a day to push hard; instead, slow down and integrate your experiences. Journaling, meditation, or simply quiet gratitude will ground you. The universe supports your reset today.

Affirmation & Gratitude

I honor my growth with gratitude, preparing for May with clarity and intention.

May 2026

Aquarius
01 May 2026

May begins with a strong focus on your inner world. Aquarius, the cosmos asks you to slow down, reflect, and check in with your emotional state. Old patterns may resurface, reminding you of lessons learned and those still to be integrated. Use today for journaling, meditation, or simply quiet time with yourself. Don't push productivity—rest is equally valuable. This pause allows you to enter May with clarity and strength. Pay attention to dreams or subtle signs—they may hold guidance.

Affirmation & Gratitude

I honor reflection and rest, trusting stillness to bring clarity and renewal as May begins.

Aquarius
02 May 2026

The Moon in your sign brings vitality and magnetism. Aquarius, today is ideal for starting fresh, setting intentions, or stepping into the spotlight. Your individuality is magnetic—others notice when you stand confidently in your truth. This is not a day to blend into the background. Speak your mind, express your creativity, and trust that your uniqueness is your superpower. Opportunities may appear when you embrace visibility and authenticity without hesitation.

Affirmation & Gratitude

I shine authentically, embracing my individuality with confidence and joy.

Aquarius
03 May 2026

Finances and resources take the spotlight today. Aquarius, review your money habits, savings, and long-term security. Are your current choices aligned with your bigger vision? Emotional triggers around money may surface—rather than ignoring them, see them as signals for change. Abundance is not only financial but also about how you manage time and energy. Align your daily decisions with your values, and you'll feel more empowered and secure.

Affirmation & Gratitude

I manage my resources wisely, aligning them with what truly supports my freedom and peace.

Aquarius
04 May 2026

Communication flows easily today. Aquarius, Mercury enhances your ability to express yourself clearly and confidently, making this a great time for writing, presenting, or networking. A conversation may spark a breakthrough or lead to an unexpected opportunity. Stay curious and receptive—insight may come from an unlikely source. Balance speaking with listening to make the most of today's energy. Your originality shines brightest when paired with clarity and openness.

Affirmation & Gratitude

I communicate with clarity and openness, trusting my words to inspire growth and opportunity.

Aquarius
05 May 2026

Emotional matters around home and family may surface. Aquarius, you may feel the need to nurture your private world—whether through creating harmony in your environment, spending time with loved ones, or resolving long-standing issues. Don't shy away from difficult conversations; healing flows more easily today when approached with compassion. Your sanctuary is your strength—when it feels stable, you can move forward with confidence in other areas of life.

Affirmation & Gratitude

I nurture harmony within my home, creating peace that supports my spirit and dreams.

Aquarius
06 May 2026

Ambition rises as your career zone is activated. Aquarius, this is a powerful day for stepping up into leadership or showcasing your unique ideas. Recognition may come for your efforts, or an opportunity may present itself. Avoid unnecessary conflict with authority figures; instead, use diplomacy to get your message across. Take one bold but strategic step toward your goals. Success comes from consistency as much as innovation.

Affirmation & Gratitude

I act with confidence and strategy, building success through originality and persistence.

Aquarius
07 May 2026

Freedom and exploration are highlighted. Aquarius, Uranus encourages you to break routine and invite change. This doesn't have to be dramatic—even small shifts bring renewal. Explore a new activity, learn something different, or connect with people outside your usual circles. Growth happens when you stretch beyond the familiar. Inspiration comes when you allow curiosity to guide you. Pay attention to unexpected insights or encounters—they may spark new directions.

Affirmation & Gratitude

I embrace change with curiosity, trusting new experiences to expand my wisdom and joy.

Aquarius
08 May 2026

Relationships come into sharper focus today. Aquarius, Venus highlights harmony but also reveals imbalances that may need addressing. If you've been giving too much or holding back, now is the time to restore equality. Honest yet compassionate conversations flow smoothly under today's energy. Partnerships thrive when both independence and connection are respected. If single, new encounters may spark interest, especially with people who appreciate your uniqueness. Professional collaborations are also favored if built on mutual respect.

Affirmation & Gratitude

I embrace balanced connections, welcoming love, respect, and freedom in all my relationships.

Aquarius
09 May 2026

The cosmos calls you inward, Aquarius. Today is best used for reflection, solitude, or spiritual practice. You may feel more sensitive than usual, so protect your energy and avoid draining situations. Dreams or intuitive nudges hold significance—write them down. This is not about withdrawal but about renewal. By tending to your inner world, you restore clarity and strength for the days ahead. Allow yourself to be still and listen to your deeper wisdom.

Affirmation & Gratitude
I honor stillness and reflection, trusting my inner guidance to renew my spirit.

Aquarius
10 May 2026

The Moon in your sign restores vitality and presence. Aquarius, today you feel magnetic and more comfortable being in the spotlight. Use this energy to start new projects, express your individuality, or simply stand confidently in who you are. Others notice when you step forward authentically. Be mindful not to push too hard—patience will ensure smoother progress. Today reminds you that your uniqueness is your most powerful gift.

Affirmation & Gratitude

I shine in my authenticity, embracing my individuality as my strength and light.

Aquarius
11 May 2026

Finances and resources are emphasized. Aquarius, review your spending and saving patterns with honesty. Are your actions supporting your long-term vision? Avoid impulsive purchases, as emotions may tempt you to spend unwisely. Instead, focus on building security and aligning choices with your values. Abundance is not just money—it's also about time, health, and emotional well-being. Today is an opportunity to shift your perspective on what truly creates freedom.

Affirmation & Gratitude

I align my financial and personal choices with values that bring lasting stability and peace.

Aquarius
12 May 2026

Mercury enhances your communication, Aquarius, making this an excellent day for sharing ideas, networking, or having meaningful conversations. A breakthrough may come through a casual exchange or an unexpected message. Stay open to inspiration—it may spark a fresh direction. Writing, teaching, or creative expression flows more easily now. Remember to balance your enthusiasm with listening, as wisdom can also come through others' perspectives. Inspiration grows when curiosity is your guide.

Affirmation & Gratitude

I communicate with clarity and openness, attracting ideas and opportunities that support growth.

Aquarius
13 May 2026

Emotional matters around home and family may require attention. Aquarius, today invites you to nurture your private world—whether through connection with loved ones, improving your environment, or finding peace within yourself. If old issues resurface, approach them with compassion. Your sanctuary is your foundation; when it feels peaceful, you thrive in other areas. Grounding yourself today helps you step more confidently into the outer world tomorrow.

Affirmation & Gratitude

I create harmony at home, nurturing stability and love as my foundation.

Aquarius
14 May 2026

Career and public life come into focus. Aquarius, opportunities for recognition or leadership may arise, asking you to step forward confidently. Your originality is valued—don't downplay it. While ambition fuels you, remember to pair boldness with diplomacy. Authority figures may test your patience, but calm confidence will win. Take one strategic step toward your bigger vision today. The seeds you plant now will bring long-term growth.

Affirmation & Gratitude

I act with confidence and wisdom, building success through authenticity and persistence.

Aquarius
15 May 2026

The cosmos stirs your adventurous side today, Aquarius. Uranus encourages you to break free from routine and seek fresh inspiration. This could mean exploring new studies, trying an unusual activity, or simply shifting your daily rhythm to welcome variety. Encounters with different people or ideas may expand your worldview. Don't resist change—embrace it as part of your growth. Allow yourself to follow curiosity, even if the path feels unconventional. Inspiration often arrives where you least expect it.

Affirmation & Gratitude

I embrace change with curiosity, trusting new experiences to guide my growth and expansion.

Aquarius
16 May 2026

Relationships take priority today, Aquarius. Venus highlights partnerships, helping you strengthen bonds while also showing where imbalances exist. Equality is key—if you've been giving too much, it's time to restore balance. Harmony comes through honesty, kindness, and mutual respect. Romantic connections feel lighter and more enjoyable now, while professional collaborations can flow smoothly. Remember, strong partnerships support your individuality rather than restrict it. Seek connections that feel natural and uplifting.

Affirmation & Gratitude

I welcome harmony and balance in my relationships, embracing love and respect in all forms.

Aquarius
17 May 2026

Reflection and inner work are favored today. Aquarius, you may feel drawn to solitude or spiritual practice, and this is where clarity emerges. Dreams or intuitive flashes may carry important messages—don't dismiss them. Old emotions may resurface, but they're ready to be acknowledged and released. This day offers quiet healing if you allow yourself space. Don't pressure yourself to be productive; growth also comes from pausing and listening inwardly.

Affirmation & Gratitude

I honor stillness and reflection, trusting my inner wisdom to guide me toward peace.

Aquarius
18 May 2026

The Moon in your sign recharges your energy, Aquarius. Today you feel magnetic, confident, and ready to step into visibility. This is the perfect day to start projects, share ideas, or simply enjoy expressing yourself authentically. Others notice when you stand tall in your truth. Be mindful of impatience—progress flows more smoothly when paired with patience. Claim your individuality boldly; your originality is your greatest strength.

Affirmation & Gratitude

I shine authentically, embracing my uniqueness with confidence and joy.

Aquarius
19 May 2026

Finances and resources are in focus. Aquarius, the cosmos is nudging you to review your relationship with abundance. Are your current choices aligned with the stability you seek? Emotional triggers around money may surface, but they are lessons in disguise. True wealth is about how you manage time, energy, and health as much as finances. Practical steps you take today will support freedom later.

Affirmation & Gratitude

I make wise choices with my resources, creating abundance that sustains freedom and balance.

Aquarius
20 May 2026

Mercury sharpens your mind and your ability to connect today, Aquarius. This is an excellent time for conversations, presentations, or negotiations. Your originality is your strongest asset, so don't water it down—say what you mean with clarity and confidence. You may receive news that shifts your perspective or sparks fresh ideas. Stay open to synchronicities; they may reveal opportunities hiding in plain sight. Communication is a two-way street, so remember to listen deeply as well.

Affirmation & Gratitude

I speak with clarity and listen with openness, trusting every exchange brings growth and opportunity.

Aquarius
21 May 2026

Emotions tied to home and family may take center stage. Aquarius, today is about nurturing your sanctuary and grounding yourself in peace. A family conversation could be healing if you approach it with compassion. If you feel restless, channel that energy into creating comfort in your living space. Your home reflects your inner world, and tending to it restores your balance. When your foundation feels stable, you're freer to pursue bigger dreams.

Affirmation & Gratitude

I create harmony within my home, nurturing peace and balance as my foundation.

Aquarius
22 May 2026

Ambition rises as your career zone is activated. Aquarius, opportunities to showcase your talents or step into leadership may appear. Don't hesitate to put your ideas forward—your originality is what sets you apart. Authority figures may challenge you, but diplomacy will win more ground than defensiveness. Take one strategic step toward your goals today. Success is about consistency, not instant results. Remember, seeds planted now grow into long-term rewards.

Affirmation & Gratitude

I step forward with confidence, building success through persistence and authenticity.

Aquarius
23 May 2026

Freedom and curiosity are the themes today. Aquarius, Uranus stirs your adventurous spirit, urging you to break away from the usual and try something new. This could mean exploring a subject you've never studied, traveling to unfamiliar places, or simply shaking up your daily rhythm. Inspiration often strikes when you leave your comfort zone. Don't resist change; embrace it as part of your evolution. Growth comes from daring to do things differently.

Affirmation & Gratitude

I embrace new experiences with curiosity, trusting change to expand my wisdom and joy.

Aquarius
24 May 2026

Partnerships come into focus under today's skies. Aquarius, Venus emphasizes connection and equality, making this a great time to deepen relationships or form new ones. If imbalance exists, you'll feel it strongly now. Have the courage to address it with honesty and kindness. Healthy connections allow freedom alongside closeness. Professional collaborations may also thrive today if built on respect and fairness. Choose relationships that uplift and support your individuality.

Affirmation & Gratitude

I welcome balanced partnerships, nurturing love and respect while honoring my independence.

Aquarius
25 May 2026

The cosmos calls you inward, Aquarius. Today is about slowing down, reflecting, and giving yourself time to recharge. Old emotions or patterns may resurface, but don't push them aside—observe and release them. Dreams or intuitive insights may bring clarity, so pay attention to subtle signs. This is not a day for overextending yourself; instead, focus on healing and renewal. Rest now prepares you for the next wave of action.

Affirmation & Gratitude

I honor rest and reflection, allowing stillness to restore my clarity and strength.

Aquarius
26 May 2026

The Moon in your sign recharges your energy, Aquarius. You feel seen, confident, and ready to step into the spotlight. Use this boost to begin projects, share your ideas, or simply express your individuality more boldly. Others are drawn to your authenticity and may offer support or recognition. Be mindful of impatience—progress takes time. Today is about owning your truth and showing the world what makes you unique.

Affirmation & Gratitude
I shine authentically, stepping forward with confidence in my individuality.

Aquarius
27 May 2026

Finances and values are highlighted today. Aquarius, you may feel called to review how you're managing your money, energy, and time. Emotional spending may tempt you, but discipline will bring more satisfaction. Abundance is not measured by possessions—it's about alignment between your values and actions. Small, practical adjustments you make today will set the stage for long-term security. The universe is asking you to honor your worth and make wise choices.

Affirmation & Gratitude

I align my resources with my values, creating stability that supports freedom and peace.

Aquarius
28 May 2026

Communication flows strongly today, Aquarius. Mercury supports your ability to share ideas with clarity and charm, making this a perfect day for networking, writing, or public speaking. A casual conversation could lead to an important opportunity, so don't dismiss small exchanges. Inspiration may come from unexpected sources, so remain open and curious. Be mindful of scattering your energy—focus on one or two priorities rather than trying to cover everything at once. Your originality makes your words impactful.

Affirmation & Gratitude

I communicate with clarity and purpose, trusting my words to inspire and attract new opportunities.

Aquarius
29 May 2026

Your home and family zone is highlighted, Aquarius. You may feel the need to nurture your private world, whether through creating comfort in your space or spending quality time with loved ones. Emotional matters may arise, but if you approach them with compassion and patience, healing can occur. Home is your sanctuary, and tending to it strengthens your foundation for everything else you want to achieve. Ground yourself today in what feels safe and true.

Affirmation & Gratitude

I nurture harmony within my home, creating peace and balance at my foundation.

Aquarius
30 May 2026

Ambition rises as your career sector is energized. Aquarius, opportunities for recognition or advancement may present themselves—don't hold back. Your originality is valued, and others notice your unique approach. If challenges arise with authority figures, respond with diplomacy rather than defensiveness. This is a day to take practical steps that align with your long-term vision. Success is not about overnight results but about building steadily over time.

Affirmation & Gratitude

I step confidently into success, trusting my originality to guide my path.

Aquarius
31 May 2026

May ends with a call for renewal and reflection. Aquarius, the cosmos invites you to review your progress and prepare for the month ahead. What have you achieved? What lessons have you learned about balance, relationships, and ambition? Today is not about pushing forward but integrating experiences. Journaling, meditation, or gratitude practice will help you close the month with peace and clarity. The universe encourages you to step into June refreshed and aligned.

Affirmation & Gratitude

I reflect with gratitude, honoring my growth and preparing for June with clarity and strength.

June
2026

Aquarius
01 June 2026

June opens with a strong focus on your networks and friendships. Aquarius, the cosmos highlights the people who inspire, support, and challenge you to grow. This is a great day to connect with groups, collaborate, or rekindle old friendships that align with your vision. Be mindful not to overextend yourself socially—quality matters more than quantity. A new opportunity may arise through a connection today, so stay open to synchronicity. Trust your instincts about who feels aligned.

Affirmation & Gratitude

I attract supportive friendships and collaborations that nurture growth, laughter, and shared purpose.

Aquarius
02 June 2026

The cosmos invites you inward for reflection. Aquarius, you may feel more sensitive than usual, craving peace and solitude. This is an ideal day to meditate, journal, or spend quiet time in nature. Old emotions may surface, but don't push them away—acknowledge and release them. Your intuition is heightened, so pay attention to dreams or subtle nudges from the universe. By giving yourself space, you prepare for the busier days ahead with renewed clarity.

Affirmation & Gratitude

I honor stillness, trusting rest and reflection to restore my strength and clarity.

Aquarius
03 June 2026

The Moon in your sign boosts your vitality and presence. Aquarius, today you feel magnetic and confident, and others are drawn to your authenticity. This is an excellent day to launch new projects, express yourself, or set intentions for personal growth. Be mindful of impatience—progress unfolds step by step. Your individuality is your strength, and when you stand unapologetically in your truth, doors open. Don't hide—today the cosmos is asking you to shine.

Affirmation & Gratitude

I shine authentically, embracing my individuality as a powerful gift.

Aquarius
04 June 2026

Finances and values are spotlighted today. Aquarius, the universe asks you to take a closer look at how you're managing money, time, and energy. Are your actions aligned with your long-term goals? Avoid impulsive spending—discipline creates security and freedom. Abundance is not just material; it's also emotional and spiritual fulfillment. Make choices today that honor your worth and your bigger picture. Even small adjustments will set the stage for long-term stability and peace.

Affirmation & Gratitude

I align my choices with my values, creating abundance that supports freedom and joy.

Aquarius
05 June 2026

Communication flows with ease today. Aquarius, Mercury enhances your ability to express ideas clearly and persuasively, making this a perfect day for writing, teaching, or negotiations. A casual conversation could open an important door, so stay receptive. Inspiration may come suddenly—capture it before it slips away. Balance speaking with listening to get the most out of interactions. This is also a favorable day for creative projects where words carry power and influence.

Affirmation & Gratitude

I communicate clearly and confidently, trusting my words to inspire and connect.

Aquarius
06 June 2026

Emotional matters connected to home and family may surface. Aquarius, you're being encouraged to nurture your private world—whether by resolving tension, creating comfort in your space, or reconnecting with loved ones. Your sanctuary is your strength, and when it feels stable, you thrive outwardly. Handle family dynamics with patience and compassion today. By tending to your roots, you create the foundation to grow toward your bigger dreams with confidence and clarity.

Affirmation & Gratitude

I nurture harmony within my home, building peace at my foundation.

Aquarius
07 June 2026

Ambition rises as your career zone activates. Aquarius, opportunities for recognition or leadership may present themselves, and it's time to step forward confidently. Your originality is your advantage—don't downplay it to fit in. Authority figures may test your patience, but calm confidence will serve you better than confrontation. This is not about overnight success but building a reputation for innovation and integrity. Take one practical step toward your goals today, no matter how small. Seeds planted now will grow steadily over time.

Affirmation & Gratitude

I step forward with confidence, trusting my originality to guide me toward lasting success.

Aquarius
08 June 2026

The cosmos encourages exploration and curiosity. Aquarius, Uranus stirs your adventurous side, making today ideal for stepping outside your comfort zone. Travel, study, or experimenting with something unusual will invigorate your spirit. Conversations with people from different backgrounds may spark fresh perspectives. Growth comes from saying yes to the unknown. Don't fear change—it's the universe expanding your horizons. Even small acts of curiosity today will ripple into larger opportunities later.

Affirmation & Gratitude

I embrace new experiences with curiosity, allowing change to expand my wisdom and joy.

Aquarius
09 June 2026

Partnerships come into focus. Aquarius, Venus emphasizes harmony but also highlights imbalances that may need addressing. If you've been giving more than receiving—or vice versa—today asks you to restore balance. This is a great time for heartfelt conversations, where honesty flows smoothly when paired with kindness. Romantic sparks may fly, or professional collaborations may deepen. Healthy connections allow individuality and freedom alongside closeness. Choose relationships that uplift and inspire.

Affirmation & Gratitude

I welcome balanced partnerships, honoring love, respect, and authenticity in all my connections.

Aquarius
10 June 2026

Introspection is favored today. Aquarius, you may feel the need for solitude or quiet reflection. Old emotions may resurface, but they are ready to be acknowledged and released. Dreams or subtle intuitive nudges carry meaning, so pay attention. Don't push productivity—renewal comes from rest and stillness. Meditation, journaling, or time in nature will bring clarity. You are being reminded that wisdom often arises when you slow down and listen inwardly.

Affirmation & Gratitude
I honor stillness and reflection, trusting inner wisdom to guide me forward.

Aquarius
11 June 2026

The Moon in your sign amplifies your energy, Aquarius. You feel magnetic, energized, and ready to step into visibility. This is a powerful day to start new projects, express yourself boldly, or simply embrace your individuality unapologetically. Others are drawn to your authenticity, and opportunities flow when you stand confidently in your truth. Be mindful of impatience—progress unfolds step by step. Today is about shining brightly without apology.

Affirmation & Gratitude

I shine in my truth, embracing my individuality as a gift to the world.

Aquarius
12 June 2026

Finances and values are highlighted today, Aquarius. The cosmos is nudging you to review how you're managing money, time, and energy. Emotional spending or impulsive choices could tempt you, but discipline will bring greater long-term peace. Abundance is not only material—it's also about balance in your health, your focus, and your relationships. Reflect on whether your daily decisions align with your bigger vision. By choosing wisely, you create stability and freedom. This is a powerful day to commit to healthier financial and personal habits.

Affirmation & Gratitude

I honor my worth and align my choices with values that create freedom, stability, and peace.

Aquarius
13 June 2026

Communication flows with ease today. Aquarius, Mercury enhances your ability to express yourself clearly, making this an excellent time for writing, teaching, or presenting your ideas. Inspiration may arrive unexpectedly through a conversation or message, so stay attentive. A casual exchange could spark a breakthrough. Balance speaking with listening—wisdom is shared both ways. Your originality shines when you express yourself authentically. Don't second-guess your words; the universe encourages you to share your perspective with confidence.

Affirmation & Gratitude

I speak my truth with clarity and confidence, trusting my words to inspire and connect.

Aquarius
14 June 2026

Emotional matters connected to home or family may rise to the surface. Aquarius, today invites you to nurture your private world—whether that's creating harmony in your space, resolving tensions, or simply enjoying comfort at home. Your sanctuary reflects your inner world, so tending to it restores balance and peace. If family conversations arise, approach them with compassion rather than defensiveness. This is a grounding day where caring for your roots will strengthen your wings for future growth.

Affirmation & Gratitude
I create harmony at home, nurturing peace and balance in my foundation.

Aquarius
15 June 2026

Your career and ambitions take center stage, Aquarius. The cosmos highlights opportunities to showcase your originality and step into leadership. Recognition is possible, but don't seek approval—focus on staying true to your vision. Challenges with authority may arise, yet diplomacy paired with confidence will carry you further than defiance. Today is about planting seeds for future growth rather than expecting immediate results. Stay consistent, and your innovation will be noticed and respected.

Affirmation & Gratitude

I act with confidence and integrity, trusting my originality to open doors to long-term success.

Aquarius
16 June 2026

Curiosity is your compass today, Aquarius. Uranus stirs your adventurous side, making you restless for change and discovery. Whether through study, travel, or exploring new ideas, expansion is calling you. Don't resist the urge to break routine—it's in new experiences that inspiration strikes. Conversations with people from different backgrounds may shift your perspective. Say yes to opportunities that push you beyond your comfort zone. Growth comes when you dare to embrace the unknown.

Affirmation & Gratitude

I welcome change with curiosity, trusting every new experience to expand my wisdom and spirit.

Aquarius
17 June 2026

Relationships are highlighted as Venus influences your chart. Aquarius, today offers harmony in love and connection, but it also asks you to notice where balance is missing. Partnerships thrive on equality—are you giving and receiving fairly? Romantic sparks may ignite, or professional collaborations may deepen if rooted in respect. Don't sacrifice your independence; true connection supports individuality. Choose relationships that uplift your spirit rather than confine it.

Affirmation & Gratitude

I honor balanced relationships, giving and receiving love with respect, honesty, and freedom.

Aquarius
18 June 2026

The cosmos calls you inward, Aquarius. This is a day for reflection, solitude, and connecting with your spiritual self. Old emotions may surface—acknowledge them with compassion rather than judgment. Rest restores your clarity, so don't pressure yourself to overachieve. Intuition is strong now; listen to subtle nudges, dreams, or signs. Healing happens when you slow down enough to hear your inner voice. Trust that this pause is preparing you for your next step.

Affirmation & Gratitude

I honor stillness, allowing inner wisdom to restore clarity and peace.

Aquarius
19 June 2026

The Moon in your sign boosts your energy, Aquarius. You feel magnetic, confident, and ready to step into visibility. This is an ideal day to express your individuality boldly—whether through creativity, conversations, or new beginnings. People are drawn to your authenticity, and opportunities may appear when you stand unapologetically in your truth. Be mindful not to rush—progress builds step by step. Your uniqueness is your greatest gift, so share it freely today.

Affirmation & Gratitude

I shine authentically, embracing my individuality with confidence and joy.

Aquarius
20 June 2026

Finances and resources take focus today. Aquarius, review your spending, savings, and overall relationship with abundance. Emotional spending may tempt you, but discipline will serve you better. Think about how you can align your resources with your long-term goals. Abundance is about more than money—it's also time, energy, and well-being. Today is an opportunity to redefine how you value yourself and your resources. Choices made now will create stability later.

Affirmation & Gratitude

I manage my resources with wisdom, aligning them with values that support freedom and peace.

Aquarius
21 June 2026

Communication is energized, Aquarius. Mercury enhances your ability to share ideas clearly, making this an excellent day for teaching, writing, or presenting. A breakthrough may come through a conversation or unexpected message. Stay curious and open—insight could appear in surprising ways. Remember to balance enthusiasm with listening, as wisdom often comes from others' perspectives. This is also a day when your originality shines through words, so don't hesitate to express yourself.

Affirmation & Gratitude

I express myself clearly and openly, trusting my words to inspire and connect.

Aquarius
22 June 2026

Emotional matters tied to home and family may surface. Aquarius, today's energy asks you to nurture your roots and strengthen your foundations. This could involve clearing your living space, reconnecting with loved ones, or addressing unresolved issues with patience. Your sanctuary reflects your inner world—when it feels balanced, so do you. Don't ignore the need for comfort and grounding. Peace at home creates the strength you need for success in other areas of life.

Affirmation & Gratitude

I nurture harmony in my home, creating peace and stability at my foundation.

Aquarius
23 June 2026

Ambition rises as your career zone is activated. Aquarius, you may feel ready to step into a leadership role or put your ideas forward with confidence. Recognition is possible, but remember to stay true to your originality. Authority figures may test your resolve—stay calm and diplomatic rather than defensive. This is a powerful day for progress if you remain steady and consistent. Take one bold step today toward your long-term goals.

Affirmation & Gratitude
I step into leadership with courage, sharing my originality with confidence and integrity.

Aquarius
24 June 2026

The cosmos stirs your adventurous spirit. Aquarius, Uranus encourages you to break free of stale routines and seek inspiration through new experiences. Travel, study, or conversations with people outside your usual circles will refresh your perspective. You may feel restless, but that's a sign of growth calling. Say yes to curiosity—it will open doors you never considered. Today is about embracing the unknown as a friend, not a threat.

Affirmation & Gratitude

I embrace new horizons, trusting curiosity and change to expand my spirit and wisdom.

Aquarius
25 June 2026

Relationships are highlighted. Aquarius, Venus emphasizes harmony, but she also shines a light on imbalance if it exists. Notice where you may be overextending or holding back. Today is perfect for heartfelt, honest conversations that restore equality. Romantic energy feels warm and inviting, while professional partnerships may flow smoothly if built on respect. Remember, connection should uplift, not confine. Surround yourself with those who support your individuality.

Affirmation & Gratitude

I welcome balanced, authentic relationships built on love, respect, and freedom.

Aquarius
26 June 2026

The cosmos draws your attention inward. Aquarius, today may feel quieter, but this is your opportunity for rest and reflection. Old emotions may bubble up—don't resist them, release them. Solitude or spiritual practices like meditation, journaling, or creative expression will bring clarity. This pause is not wasted—it's your reset button. By evening, you'll feel lighter and more aligned. Trust the healing power of stillness.

Affirmation & Gratitude

I honor quiet reflection, trusting it to renew my clarity and strength.

Aquarius
27 June 2026

The Moon in your sign brings vitality, Aquarius. You feel magnetic and ready to take bold steps forward. This is an excellent day to launch projects, set intentions, or embrace your individuality more openly. Others notice when you stand confidently in your truth. Be mindful of impatience—progress requires steady pacing. Your originality is your strength; when you express it unapologetically, you inspire those around you.

Affirmation & Gratitude

I shine authentically, embracing my uniqueness as a gift to the world.

Aquarius
28 June 2026

Finances and resources come into focus. Aquarius, the cosmos urges you to take an honest look at how you're managing money, time, and energy. Emotional spending or quick fixes may tempt you, but the lesson today is discipline. Think long-term security and how your daily choices support freedom. Abundance is about more than material wealth—it's also emotional fulfillment and peace of mind. Consider whether your resources are flowing toward what truly matters. Aligning values with actions will create stability.

Affirmation & Gratitude

I manage my resources with wisdom, building stability that nurtures both freedom and peace.

Aquarius
29 June 2026

Communication is highlighted, Aquarius. Mercury enhances your ability to share your ideas with clarity, charm, and originality. This is a powerful day for writing, teaching, or having meaningful conversations. Inspiration may come through a casual exchange or unexpected message, so stay alert. Be mindful not to scatter your focus—choose one or two key areas to direct your energy. Your words carry influence today; speak with confidence and authenticity, and the right people will listen.

Affirmation & Gratitude

I express myself clearly and authentically, trusting my words to inspire and connect.

Aquarius
30 June 2026

June ends with a call for reflection and integration. Aquarius, take time to review the month's lessons and acknowledge your growth. Where have you honored your individuality? Where have you been called to adjust your values or relationships? Celebrate your progress, even the small steps, because they've brought you here. Today is ideal for journaling, meditation, or gratitude practice. Reflection ensures you step into July with clarity, alignment, and renewed purpose.

Affirmation & Gratitude

I reflect with gratitude, honoring my growth and preparing for July with clarity and intention.

July 2026

Aquarius
01 July 2026

July begins with a focus on your inner well-being, Aquarius. The cosmos is encouraging you to slow down and check in with yourself. After a busy June, your body and spirit may crave rest. Pay attention to your health, both physical and emotional. This is a day to nurture routines that support balance—eat well, move gently, and give yourself permission to recharge. You don't need to push hard to prove your worth; restoration will fuel your creativity and drive in the weeks ahead.

Affirmation & Gratitude

I honor my body and spirit, allowing rest and balance to restore my energy.

Aquarius
02 July 2026

Relationships take the spotlight today. Aquarius, Venus emphasizes connection, love, and harmony. If you're in a partnership, this is a day to strengthen bonds through honesty and shared joy. If single, new opportunities for connection may appear, especially through social or professional settings. Remember that balanced relationships thrive on equality—don't overgive or hold back. Let authenticity guide you, and you'll attract connections that honor both freedom and closeness.

Affirmation & Gratitude

I welcome love and harmony, nurturing relationships that support freedom, respect, and joy.

Aquarius
03 July 2026

Introspection calls as the cosmos draws your attention inward. Aquarius, today may feel quieter, but this is an opportunity to reconnect with your deeper self. Emotions may surface, but they are signals, not burdens. Reflection, journaling, or spiritual practices will bring clarity. Don't force productivity—true progress comes from understanding where you've been and what you're ready to release. Allow yourself the gift of stillness, and trust the guidance that comes through your intuition.

Affirmation & Gratitude

I honor stillness and reflection, trusting my inner wisdom to guide me.

Aquarius
04 July 2026

The Moon in your sign brings a surge of vitality and confidence. Aquarius, you feel magnetic today, and others notice your authenticity. This is an excellent time to begin new projects, share your ideas, or simply step into your individuality more boldly. Be mindful not to become impatient with slower-moving people—focus on your own path. Today the universe is reminding you that your uniqueness is your greatest strength. Shine unapologetically.

Affirmation & Gratitude

I shine authentically, embracing my individuality with courage and joy.

Aquarius
05 July 2026

Finances and resources are emphasized. Aquarius, today is ideal for reviewing your budget, investments, or daily routines that affect your stability. Emotional triggers around money may arise, but don't ignore them—they highlight where adjustments are needed. Abundance is about more than possessions—it's about using resources wisely to create freedom and peace. Small, practical steps today will have lasting results. Align your decisions with your higher values for true security.

Affirmation & Gratitude

I make wise choices with my resources, creating stability that supports freedom and peace.

Aquarius
06 July 2026

Communication flows effortlessly today. Aquarius, Mercury enhances your ability to express yourself clearly and persuasively. This is a great time for presentations, writing, or meaningful conversations. Someone may share insight that shifts your perspective or sparks fresh inspiration. Stay open to unexpected opportunities through dialogue. Your originality makes your words impactful, so speak authentically. Remember, wisdom comes not only from talking but also from listening deeply.

Affirmation & Gratitude

I communicate with clarity and openness, trusting my words to inspire and connect.

Aquarius
07 July 2026

Home and family matters come into focus. Aquarius, today is about nurturing your sanctuary and ensuring your environment feels like a source of peace. If tensions arise within family, approach with patience and compassion. Creating balance in your personal space supports your emotional well-being. Simple actions like reorganizing, decorating, or spending quality time with loved ones can make a big difference. Your inner world strengthens when your foundations feel secure.

Affirmation & Gratitude

I nurture harmony within my home, creating peace and stability at my roots.

Aquarius
08 July 2026

Career and ambition are spotlighted today. Aquarius, you may feel ready to step forward and take charge of a project or showcase your talents. Recognition could arrive, but it's more important that you stay true to your vision. Challenges from authority figures may test your patience, but diplomacy will carry your message further than defiance. Progress is built step by step, so focus on consistent effort rather than overnight results. Trust that your originality is valued and needed.

Affirmation & Gratitude

I step into leadership with confidence, trusting my originality to create lasting impact.

Aquarius
09 July 2026

Curiosity guides you today, Aquarius. Uranus stirs your adventurous side, making this a perfect day to try something new or seek inspiration outside your comfort zone. Whether it's exploring new knowledge, connecting with different cultures, or simply changing your routine, growth happens when you allow variety into your life. Encounters today may open your eyes to fresh perspectives. The universe is asking you to embrace change as a friend, not a disruption.

Affirmation & Gratitude

I welcome change with curiosity, trusting new experiences to expand my wisdom and spirit.

Aquarius
10 July 2026

Relationships come into focus under Venus's influence. Aquarius, today is about balance in connection. Are you overgiving or holding back? Equality is the foundation of healthy bonds, and the cosmos is encouraging you to address imbalance honestly. Romantic connections feel supported now, while friendships and professional partnerships can deepen if mutual respect is present. Love should never restrict—it should uplift and allow freedom. Choose the connections that reflect authenticity and joy.

Affirmation & Gratitude

I nurture balanced relationships, giving and receiving love with honesty and respect.

Aquarius
11 July 2026

The cosmos calls you inward today. Aquarius, you may feel the need for solitude or spiritual reflection. Old memories or emotions could surface, reminding you of lessons yet to be integrated. Don't resist them—honor their message and release what no longer serves you. Intuition is heightened, so pay attention to dreams, subtle signs, or inner nudges. Rest is valuable; it is preparing you for the next phase of action.

Affirmation & Gratitude

I honor stillness and reflection, trusting my intuition to guide me forward with clarity.

Aquarius
12 July 2026

The Moon in your sign amplifies your energy and charisma. Aquarius, today you feel magnetic and more comfortable stepping into visibility. This is a wonderful day to share your ideas, start projects, or simply embrace your individuality more boldly. Others are drawn to your authenticity, and opportunities may arise through your confidence. Be patient—progress builds steadily when fueled by trust in yourself. Your originality is your greatest gift; share it freely.

Affirmation & Gratitude

I shine authentically, embracing my individuality with confidence and joy.

Aquarius
13 July 2026

Finances and values take priority. Aquarius, today's energy supports budgeting, reviewing investments, or clarifying your relationship with abundance. Emotional spending may tempt you, but the universe asks for discipline. Abundance is more than material wealth—it includes peace of mind, time, and energy. Align your financial and personal decisions with your higher goals. Choices made today will support long-term stability and freedom.

Affirmation & Gratitude

I align my resources with my values, creating stability that sustains freedom and peace.

Aquarius
14 July 2026

Communication is highlighted today. Aquarius, Mercury enhances your ability to express ideas clearly and persuasively, making this a powerful time for teaching, presenting, or sharing your insights. Inspiration may come through an unexpected message or a casual conversation. Don't scatter your energy—focus your words where they matter most. Authenticity will ensure your message resonates. Listening is just as important as speaking; wisdom flows both ways.

Affirmation & Gratitude

I express myself with clarity and authenticity, trusting my words to inspire meaningful connection.

Aquarius
15 July 2026

Emotional matters around home and family rise to the surface today, Aquarius. You may feel the need to nurture your private world, whether by creating harmony in your space, spending time with loved ones, or addressing past tensions. Don't shy away from sensitive conversations—compassion and patience will open doors to healing. Your sanctuary is a reflection of your inner world, and by tending to it, you strengthen your spirit. The cosmos reminds you that peace at home fuels confidence in the outer world.

Affirmation & Gratitude

I create harmony within my home, nurturing peace and stability at my foundation.

Aquarius
16 July 2026

Ambition and recognition come into focus. Aquarius, the cosmos is asking you to step up and show your capabilities in professional or public life. Opportunities to showcase your originality may appear, but they require confidence. Authority figures might challenge you, but remain calm and steady. Bold yet diplomatic action will lead to respect and progress. Today isn't about instant success but laying down strong building blocks for the future. Trust that your innovative spirit is noticed.

Affirmation & Gratitude
I step into leadership with courage, sharing my originality with confidence and integrity.

Aquarius
17 July 2026

The cosmos stirs your adventurous side, Aquarius. Uranus encourages you to break away from routine and embrace variety. This could be as simple as exploring a new hobby, studying something unusual, or connecting with people outside your usual circles. Growth is calling you, and it arrives when you step into the unknown. Inspiration may come through unexpected encounters, so say yes to invitations that spark curiosity. Change is not disruption—it is opportunity.

Affirmation & Gratitude

I embrace new experiences with curiosity, allowing change to expand my wisdom and joy.

Aquarius
18 July 2026

Relationships are spotlighted today. Venus brings harmony and warmth, but she also reveals where imbalance may exist. If you've been giving more than you receive, or withholding your truth, it's time to address it. Connection should uplift both sides, not drain one. Conversations flow more smoothly now, and honesty paired with kindness will strengthen bonds. Choose partnerships that celebrate individuality while encouraging closeness.

Affirmation & Gratitude

I welcome balanced relationships, embracing love and respect in all my connections.

Aquarius
19 July 2026

The cosmos encourages introspection today. Aquarius, your energy may feel lower, but this is a gift—it allows you to pause and reflect. Old memories or emotions may resurface, but they are guiding you to release what no longer serves. Journaling, meditation, or quiet time in nature will help you process. Don't force productivity; inner clarity is more important than outer progress today. Trust that silence carries answers you've been seeking.

Affirmation & Gratitude
I honor rest and reflection, trusting stillness to restore my clarity and peace.

Aquarius
20 July 2026

The Moon in your sign boosts vitality and confidence. Aquarius, today you're magnetic, and others are drawn to your authenticity. This is an excellent time to begin projects, assert your individuality, or step into new opportunities. Progress may feel exciting but pace yourself—steady effort ensures lasting results. When you own your truth unapologetically, you open doors and inspire others to do the same. This is a day to shine brightly without hesitation.

Affirmation & Gratitude

I shine authentically, embracing my individuality as my greatest strength.

Aquarius
21 July 2026

Finances and resources take the spotlight today. Aquarius, review your spending, saving, and long-term planning. Are your choices aligned with your higher vision? Emotional triggers around money may appear, but see them as lessons rather than burdens. Abundance is not just financial—it is also time, health, and peace of mind. Small but steady steps today can build the stability you desire. The universe is reminding you to honor your worth through wise decisions.

Affirmation & Gratitude

I manage my resources with wisdom, creating stability that sustains freedom and peace.

Aquarius
22 July 2026

Communication is emphasized today, Aquarius. Mercury enhances your ability to express yourself with clarity and originality. This is an excellent time for writing, presenting, or having meaningful conversations. A casual discussion could lead to a breakthrough or opportunity, so pay attention to synchronicities. Be careful not to scatter your focus—direct your energy toward one or two key priorities. Your words hold influence now, so speak authentically and confidently. Balance talking with listening, as wisdom often flows both ways.

Affirmation & Gratitude

I express myself clearly and authentically, trusting my words to inspire connection and opportunity.

Aquarius
23 July 2026

Family and home take priority today. Aquarius, you may feel pulled toward your private world, craving comfort, or tending to unfinished matters in your sanctuary. Emotional dynamics with loved ones may arise—approach with patience and compassion. The universe asks you to create peace at your foundation so you can thrive outwardly. Simple actions like reorganizing, decorating, or enjoying quality time with family will ground your energy and restore balance.

Affirmation & Gratitude

I nurture harmony at home, creating a sanctuary that restores peace and stability.

Aquarius
24 July 2026

Career matters rise to the surface. Aquarius, opportunities to showcase your leadership or creativity may present themselves. Recognition is possible, but don't measure your value solely by others' approval—stay aligned with your vision. Challenges with authority figures may appear, but diplomacy will serve you better than confrontation. Take one steady, practical step that supports your bigger goals. Success today comes through confidence paired with strategy.

Affirmation & Gratitude

I step confidently into success, trusting my originality to guide long-term achievements.

Aquarius
25 July 2026

Uranus sparks your adventurous side, Aquarius, pushing you to break free from stale routines. This is a great day to explore, whether through travel, learning, or simply trying something new. Unexpected encounters could shift your perspective and inspire fresh goals. Restlessness is a sign that you're ready to expand. Don't resist change—embrace it as an ally. Growth arrives when you lean into new experiences, even small ones.

Affirmation & Gratitude

I embrace change with curiosity, trusting new experiences to expand my wisdom and joy.

Aquarius
26 July 2026

Relationships are spotlighted today. Aquarius, Venus encourages harmony, but she also reveals where imbalances may exist. If you've been giving more than you're receiving, or avoiding honesty, this is your chance to restore equality. Authentic connection flourishes when both sides feel valued. Romantic sparks may fly, or professional collaborations may strengthen. Focus on building partnerships that celebrate individuality while encouraging mutual respect and support.

Affirmation & Gratitude

I welcome balanced partnerships, honoring love, trust, and freedom in all my connections.

Aquarius
27 July 2026

Introspection and healing take center stage. Aquarius, the cosmos encourages you to retreat from busyness and reconnect with your inner world. Old emotions may resurface—rather than resisting, acknowledge and release them. Quiet time spent journaling, meditating, or walking in nature will bring clarity. Your intuition is sharp now; listen carefully to subtle nudges. Rest is not avoidance—it's preparation. Trust that slowing down today will fuel your future steps with renewed strength.

Affirmation & Gratitude

I honor rest and reflection, trusting stillness to bring clarity and renewal.

Aquarius
28 July 2026

The Moon in your sign amplifies your vitality, Aquarius. You feel magnetic, expressive, and ready to step into visibility. This is a powerful day to set intentions, share your talents, or start something new. Be careful not to rush—progress flows better when steady. Your individuality shines brightest when you embrace it fully, without apology. Today is about celebrating your uniqueness and letting the world see your true colors.

Affirmation & Gratitude

I shine authentically, embracing my individuality as my greatest strength.

Aquarius
29 July 2026

Finances and values come into focus. Aquarius, review your relationship with abundance—are your actions aligned with your long-term security? Emotional spending could tempt you, but the cosmos asks for discipline and wisdom. True wealth is not only financial—it includes time, peace, and energy. Small steps taken today to manage your resources will bring greater stability and freedom later. See money as a tool, not a measure of self-worth.

Affirmation & Gratitude

I align my resources with wisdom, creating stability that sustains freedom and peace.

Aquarius
30 July 2026

Communication is energized. Aquarius, Mercury sharpens your intellect, helping you connect meaningfully with others. This is a great day for teaching, writing, or presenting ideas. Inspiration may come through an unexpected message or conversation—stay receptive. Authenticity makes your words impactful, so don't dilute your truth to fit others' expectations. Balance your enthusiasm with deep listening to make the most of today's energy.

Affirmation & Gratitude

I communicate with clarity and openness, trusting my words to inspire and connect.

Aquarius
31 July 2026

July closes with a call for reflection and gratitude. Aquarius, the cosmos invites you to review the past month's progress and acknowledge your growth. Where have you embraced change? Where have you strengthened balance in relationships, career, or self-worth? Celebrate even the small victories. Today is ideal for journaling, meditation, or simply giving thanks for how far you've come. Reflection ensures you step into August aligned and prepared for fresh beginnings.

Affirmation & Gratitude

I reflect with gratitude, honoring my growth and preparing for August with clarity and strength.

August
2026

Aquarius
01 August 2026

August begins with energy focused on your relationships. Aquarius, the cosmos highlights balance in partnerships, both romantic and professional. You may feel called to deepen a bond or address areas where equality is missing. Honest and compassionate conversations are easier now, so don't shy away from them. If single, this energy may attract people who resonate with your individuality. Remember: authentic love uplifts rather than restricts. Partnerships today can become stronger foundations for the months ahead.

Affirmation & Gratitude

I welcome balanced relationships, embracing love, respect, and freedom in all my connections.

Aquarius
02 August 2026

Introspection is favored today. Aquarius, you may feel more sensitive than usual, craving peace and quiet to process emotions. Don't dismiss old memories or resurfacing feelings—they're reminders of what needs to be released. Journaling, meditation, or solitude will bring clarity and healing. This is not a day for pushing forward aggressively, but for honoring stillness and trusting your intuition. Rest today prepares you for upcoming opportunities. Listen to your inner voice; it knows the way.

Affirmation & Gratitude

I honor stillness and reflection, trusting my inner wisdom to bring clarity and renewal.

Aquarius
03 August 2026

The Moon in your sign revitalizes you, Aquarius. You feel magnetic, energized, and ready to take bold steps. This is a wonderful time to start projects, share your vision, or simply embrace your individuality more confidently. Others notice your authenticity, and opportunities may flow when you express yourself openly. Be mindful of impatience—progress comes steadily, not all at once. The universe encourages you to shine unapologetically and show the world your unique brilliance.

Affirmation & Gratitude

I shine authentically, embracing my individuality with confidence and joy.

Aquarius
04 August 2026

Finances and resources take the spotlight today. Aquarius, review how your money, time, and energy are being managed. Are your current choices building the stability you want long-term? Emotional spending may tempt you, but discipline will serve you better. Abundance is more than possessions —it includes health, time, and peace of mind. Realign your decisions with your true values. Today is an excellent day to plant seeds for lasting financial and personal security.

Affirmation & Gratitude

I manage my resources with wisdom, creating stability that supports freedom and peace.

Aquarius
05 August 2026

Communication flows effortlessly, Aquarius. Mercury sharpens your intellect, making this a great time for writing, presenting, or meaningful discussions. A casual conversation could spark inspiration or even lead to an unexpected opportunity. Stay open to new ideas and don't be afraid to express yourself. Your originality makes your words impactful. Listening deeply is just as important as speaking today. Knowledge is exchanged when conversations are authentic and respectful.

Affirmation & Gratitude

I speak with clarity and listen with openness, trusting my words to inspire and connect.

Aquarius
06 August 2026

Home and family matters rise to the surface. Aquarius, the cosmos asks you to nurture your sanctuary and strengthen your foundations. This may mean addressing family dynamics, creating harmony in your space, or tending to your emotional roots. If tensions arise, patience and compassion will bring resolution. A peaceful home supports your dreams and ambitions. By grounding yourself today, you'll feel more secure to embrace opportunities ahead.

Affirmation & Gratitude
I create harmony within my home, building peace and stability at my foundation.

Aquarius
07 August 2026

Ambition rises as your career sector activates. Aquarius, today is about stepping forward with confidence and allowing your originality to shine in professional settings. Recognition is possible, but don't rely solely on others' approval—stay aligned with your vision. Authority figures may test your resolve; handle challenges with diplomacy. Progress comes from strategic, consistent effort rather than dramatic leaps. The seeds you plant now will support future success.

Affirmation & Gratitude

I step forward with confidence, building success through authenticity and persistence.

Aquarius
08 August 2026

Curiosity calls today, Aquarius. Uranus stirs your adventurous side, making this a perfect time to seek new experiences or explore fresh perspectives. Growth doesn't always require dramatic change—it can come through small adjustments like learning a new skill, connecting with someone different, or shifting your routine. Conversations may open unexpected doors, so stay open. Restlessness is a sign you're ready to expand beyond your current boundaries. Trust the new paths appearing.

Affirmation & Gratitude

I embrace new horizons with curiosity, trusting change to expand my wisdom and joy.

Aquarius
09 August 2026

Relationships take center stage. Aquarius, Venus highlights harmony, but she also brings awareness to imbalances. If you've been giving too much or holding back your truth, today encourages you to restore equality. Romantic sparks may feel stronger now, and professional collaborations thrive when respect is mutual. Choose partnerships that uplift and empower your individuality rather than restrict it. Connection today can deepen meaningfully when built on honesty and balance.

Affirmation & Gratitude

I welcome balanced connections, embracing love, respect, and freedom in my relationships.

Aquarius
10 August 2026

Introspection and healing are encouraged. Aquarius, the cosmos draws your focus inward, asking you to slow down and tend to your spirit. Old emotions may surface, but they bring wisdom if you allow yourself to listen. Solitude, journaling, or meditation will reveal clarity. Don't push for productivity today—progress is found in reflection and release. Trust that your intuition is sharper now; pay attention to subtle nudges, signs, and dreams.

Affirmation & Gratitude

I honor stillness and reflection, trusting my intuition to bring guidance and peace.

Aquarius
11 August 2026

The Moon in your sign brings a burst of vitality, Aquarius. You feel magnetic, energized, and ready to take bold steps. Today is ideal for starting projects, asserting your individuality, or simply enjoying being seen for who you truly are. Others are drawn to your authenticity, and opportunities may appear when you stand confidently in your truth. Be patient with progress; step-by-step consistency ensures lasting results. Shine brightly without hesitation.

Affirmation & Gratitude

I shine authentically, embracing my individuality as my greatest strength.

Aquarius
12 August 2026

Finances and values come into focus today. Aquarius, you may feel called to review your spending habits and investments. Emotional triggers around money may surface, but they're here to guide you into wiser decisions. Abundance is not just material—it's also about the way you honor your energy, health, and time. Align choices with your long-term vision, and you'll create stability that supports freedom. Small adjustments now create lasting results.

Affirmation & Gratitude

I make wise choices with my resources, creating abundance that sustains freedom and peace.

Aquarius
13 August 2026

Communication is favored under today's skies. Aquarius, Mercury sharpens your mind, giving you the ability to convey your ideas clearly and persuasively. This is a great day for writing, teaching, or engaging in meaningful conversations. A casual exchange may bring unexpected inspiration or opportunity. Be mindful not to scatter your attention—focus your energy where it matters most. Authenticity will ensure your words resonate deeply with those who hear them.

Affirmation & Gratitude

I speak with clarity and confidence, trusting my words to create meaningful impact.

Aquarius
14 August 2026

Home and family matters come to the forefront. Aquarius, the cosmos encourages you to nurture your private world. This could mean resolving family dynamics, beautifying your space, or simply creating a sense of peace in your environment. Don't ignore emotional needs—your sanctuary is your foundation, and when it feels stable, you flourish outwardly. Today is about creating comfort and balance in your personal life. Grounding yourself here brings strength for future growth.

Affirmation & Gratitude

I nurture peace at home, building harmony and stability at my roots.

Aquarius
15 August 2026

Your career and ambitions come into sharp focus today, Aquarius. The cosmos encourages you to step up and claim your space in professional or public life. Opportunities for recognition may present themselves, but they require confidence and persistence. Authority figures may challenge you, so approach situations with diplomacy rather than defensiveness. Success now is built on steady effort and your ability to remain authentic while still being strategic. Today is about showing that originality is your strongest asset in leadership.

Affirmation & Gratitude

I act with confidence and integrity, knowing my originality is my key to success.

Aquarius
16 August 2026

Curiosity sparks your adventurous side, Aquarius. Uranus stirs your desire to break away from the ordinary, making this a perfect day for exploration. You may feel drawn to learn something new, travel, or connect with people who expand your worldview. Inspiration often arrives when you step outside your comfort zone, so don't resist opportunities for change. Growth is calling, and the universe is encouraging you to follow your curiosity without hesitation.

Affirmation & Gratitude

I welcome new experiences with curiosity, trusting exploration to expand my wisdom and joy.

Aquarius
17 August 2026

Relationships are emphasized today. Venus encourages harmony and connection, but she also reveals where imbalance may exist. Pay attention to how much you're giving or receiving. Healthy connections support freedom as much as closeness. If partnered, open conversations strengthen your bond. If single, you may attract someone who values your individuality. Professional collaborations are favored when built on fairness and respect. Choose bonds that uplift you rather than restrict you.

Affirmation & Gratitude

I nurture balanced relationships, honoring love, freedom, and respect in all connections.

Aquarius
18 August 2026

Introspection is highlighted. Aquarius, the cosmos invites you to step back, slow down, and listen to your inner voice. Old emotions or patterns may resurface—acknowledge them, then release what no longer serves. Solitude, meditation, or journaling will restore clarity. This is not a day for outward achievement but for inward growth. Trust that this pause is necessary; it allows you to recharge and realign your energy with your greater vision.

Affirmation & Gratitude
I honor rest and reflection, allowing inner stillness to restore clarity and peace.

Aquarius
19 August 2026

The Moon in your sign gives you a boost of vitality and presence. Aquarius, today is perfect for embracing your individuality and stepping into visibility. Begin a project, set intentions, or simply let your uniqueness shine. Others are drawn to your authenticity, and opportunities may appear when you confidently share your truth. Be mindful of impatience—progress is steady, not instant. Today is about owning who you are without hesitation.

Affirmation & Gratitude

I shine authentically, embracing my individuality as my greatest gift.

Aquarius
20 August 2026

Finances and values demand attention today. Aquarius, review your money habits, savings, or investments with honesty. Avoid impulsive spending—choose stability over temporary gratification. True abundance is not only about possessions but also about emotional security, health, and time. Ask yourself whether your actions align with your higher goals. Small, practical adjustments today will lead to greater freedom and stability down the line. Value yourself enough to make wise choices.

Affirmation & Gratitude

I manage my resources wisely, creating stability that sustains my freedom and peace.

Aquarius
21 August 2026

Communication flows effortlessly. Aquarius, Mercury boosts your ability to share ideas and connect meaningfully with others. This is an excellent day for writing, teaching, or engaging in important discussions. A casual chat may spark inspiration or bring an unexpected opportunity. Stay open to dialogue, but focus your energy on what matters most. Authenticity ensures your words resonate deeply. Balance speaking with active listening to make the most of today's cosmic energy.

Affirmation & Gratitude

I speak my truth with clarity and listen with openness, trusting every exchange to inspire growth.

Aquarius
22 August 2026

Emotional matters around home and family rise to the surface today, Aquarius. You may feel called to nurture your private world—whether through reconnecting with loved ones, creating balance in your environment, or resolving old issues. The cosmos encourages you to prioritize peace at your foundation. When your inner sanctuary feels calm, you are stronger in the outer world. Compassion and patience are your greatest tools today. Don't underestimate the power of small gestures in restoring harmony.

Affirmation & Gratitude

I create harmony at home, nurturing peace and stability at my roots.

Aquarius
23 August 2026

Ambition surges as your career zone activates. Aquarius, opportunities for recognition or leadership may arise, and it's time to step into your power with confidence. Your originality is your strength—don't water it down to fit expectations. Authority figures may test your resolve, but diplomacy and clarity will help you navigate challenges. Remember, consistency matters more than speed. Each step you take now builds the foundation for long-term success.

Affirmation & Gratitude

I step confidently into leadership, trusting my originality to guide me forward.

Aquarius
24 August 2026

Curiosity stirs your adventurous side today. Aquarius, Uranus encourages you to break out of routine and explore something new. This might be through study, travel, or connecting with people who inspire fresh ideas. Growth often comes from stepping outside your comfort zone, and today the universe is pushing you to do just that. Inspiration may strike suddenly, so remain open and flexible. Say yes to what excites your spirit.

Affirmation & Gratitude
I embrace new experiences with curiosity, trusting change to expand my wisdom and joy.

Aquarius
25 August 2026

Relationships are spotlighted. Aquarius, Venus highlights harmony but also brings awareness to imbalances. Are you giving too much, or holding back your truth? Today is a chance to restore equality. Romantic energy feels warm, while professional collaborations thrive if rooted in respect. Choose connections that uplift and support your individuality rather than restrict it. The cosmos reminds you that true love and partnership never ask you to dim your light.

Affirmation & Gratitude

I nurture balanced, authentic relationships built on love, trust, and freedom.

Aquarius
26 August 2026

The cosmos calls for introspection. Aquarius, today is best spent in reflection and renewal. Old emotions may resurface, but they carry lessons. Don't resist—allow yourself to process and release them. Rest, journaling, or meditation will provide clarity. This is not about outward productivity but inner healing. Trust that this pause is preparing you for greater momentum ahead. Solitude today brings the insight you've been seeking.

Affirmation & Gratitude

I honor stillness and reflection, trusting inner wisdom to restore clarity and peace.

Aquarius
27 August 2026

The Moon in your sign energizes you, Aquarius. Today you feel magnetic and alive, ready to express yourself boldly. This is a day to begin new projects, set intentions, or simply step into your individuality without hesitation. Others are drawn to your authenticity, and opportunities may appear when you stand unapologetically in your truth. Be mindful of impatience—progress grows with steady effort. Shine brightly today; the cosmos supports your confidence.

Affirmation & Gratitude

I shine authentically, embracing my individuality with courage and joy.

Aquarius
28 August 2026

Finances and resources take the spotlight. Aquarius, review your budget, savings, or investments with honesty. Emotional triggers around money may arise, but they guide you toward wiser decisions. Abundance is not only financial—it's also time, health, and emotional balance. Align your choices with your higher goals to build long-term security. Even small steps today can create lasting freedom and stability. Value yourself by valuing your resources.

Affirmation & Gratitude

I manage my resources wisely, creating stability that sustains my freedom and peace.

Aquarius
29 August 2026

Communication flows easily today. Aquarius, Mercury helps you express yourself with clarity and originality. This is an excellent time for presentations, writing, or important conversations. A casual discussion may spark a breakthrough, so stay alert for insights. Authenticity is key—speak your truth with confidence, and your words will resonate. Balance enthusiasm with listening; wisdom often arrives through others' perspectives. Today your voice carries extra influence, so use it well.

Affirmation & Gratitude

I express myself with clarity and confidence, trusting my words to inspire meaningful connection.

Aquarius
30 August 2026

Home and family matters come to the forefront. Aquarius, you may feel called to strengthen your foundations by creating peace in your living environment or reconnecting with loved ones. If tensions arise, approach them with patience and compassion. Your sanctuary reflects your inner world; when it feels balanced, you flourish in other areas. Today is about grounding yourself emotionally, so you can feel secure stepping into what lies ahead.

Affirmation & Gratitude

I create peace and harmony at home, nurturing stability as my foundation.

Aquarius
31 August 2026

August ends with a reflective yet empowering tone, Aquarius. The cosmos invites you to pause and look back over the past month with gratitude and honesty. Where have you stepped into your authenticity? Where have you been challenged to rebalance relationships, finances, or ambitions? Today is about integration—taking the lessons you've gathered and using them as fuel for September's fresh start. This is not about dwelling on mistakes but celebrating growth, even in small steps. Journaling, meditation, or a gratitude ritual will anchor your insights. Honor how far you've come.

Affirmation & Gratitude

I reflect with gratitude, honoring my growth and preparing for September with cl

September 2026

Aquarius
01 September 2026

September begins with a focus on shared resources and deeper emotional truths. Aquarius, the cosmos highlights areas of give-and-take in your life, whether financial, emotional, or energetic. You may be called to examine how balanced these exchanges feel. Are you investing your time and energy in places that truly serve your higher goals? Conversations about money, intimacy, or trust may arise, offering an opportunity for healing. Transparency brings growth. This is a day to face truths with courage, knowing honesty clears space for empowerment and renewal.

Affirmation & Gratitude

I embrace honesty and balance, allowing trust and transparency to strengthen my foundations.

Aquarius
02 September 2026

The cosmos stirs your curiosity, Aquarius. Today you may feel a strong urge to learn, explore, or stretch beyond your current boundaries. Whether through study, travel, or engaging with new ideas, the energy supports expansion. Unexpected conversations may spark inspiration, shifting your outlook in profound ways. Embrace the unusual—it could provide the breakthrough you've been waiting for. The universe reminds you that freedom and growth often arrive when you're willing to see the world differently.

Affirmation & Gratitude

I welcome fresh perspectives, trusting new ideas to expand my wisdom and spirit.

Aquarius
03 September 2026

Partnerships are in the spotlight today. Aquarius, Venus highlights love, harmony, and collaboration. Romantic bonds feel especially warm and supportive, while professional relationships can flourish if rooted in fairness. If imbalance has been building, you may feel it strongly today. Instead of ignoring it, address it with compassion and clarity. Authentic partnerships encourage freedom alongside closeness. Trust that when you show up as your true self, the right people will meet you there.

Affirmation & Gratitude

I cultivate balanced relationships, giving and receiving love with honesty, respect, and joy.

Aquarius
04 September 2026

The cosmos pulls your attention inward, Aquarius. Today is best used for reflection, healing, and stillness. Old memories or emotions may surface, but they're surfacing for release, not to hold you back. Solitude will restore clarity, so take time to journal, meditate, or simply rest. This is not a day for forcing productivity but for honoring your inner world. Wisdom often comes in whispers—listen carefully. Trust that slowing down now sets you up for greater strength later.

Affirmation & Gratitude

I honor stillness, trusting rest and reflection to renew my clarity and strength.

Aquarius
05 September 2026

The Moon in your sign recharges your energy and confidence, Aquarius. You feel magnetic, alive, and ready to express yourself boldly. This is a great day to start new projects, set intentions, or share your vision with others. Opportunities may arise when you stand unapologetically in your truth. Be mindful of impatience—progress builds over time, not overnight. The universe is encouraging you to step fully into visibility and embrace your uniqueness as a gift.

Affirmation & Gratitude

I shine authentically, embracing my individuality as my source of strength and joy.

Aquarius
06 September 2026

Finances and values take focus. Aquarius, today is ideal for reviewing your relationship with abundance. Are your money habits supporting your long-term dreams, or are they creating unnecessary stress? Emotional spending may tempt you, but the cosmos urges discipline. True wealth is not just money—it's time, health, and peace of mind. Realign your daily choices with your bigger vision, and stability will follow. Small steps now set the stage for freedom later.

Affirmation & Gratitude

I align my resources with my values, creating abundance that sustains freedom and balance.

Aquarius
07 September 2026

Communication flows smoothly today. Aquarius, Mercury helps you express yourself clearly and persuasively, making this a wonderful time for writing, teaching, or networking. Inspiration may come through an unexpected conversation or message—stay open to it. Authenticity ensures your words resonate. Balance enthusiasm with listening, as wisdom may arrive through others' insights. Today is about exchanging knowledge in a way that uplifts and inspires. Speak your truth and allow dialogue to spark new growth.

Affirmation & Gratitude

I share my words with clarity and confidence, trusting communication to bring inspiration and connection.

Aquarius
08 September 2026

Home and family matters take priority today, Aquarius. The cosmos urges you to nurture your sanctuary, whether through tending to your physical space or addressing emotional dynamics with loved ones. A family discussion may arise, offering an opportunity for healing if approached with patience and compassion. Don't ignore your need for grounding—your private life is the root from which your public life grows. Creating peace in your environment helps you feel balanced, strong, and supported in every other area of life.

Affirmation & Gratitude

I create peace within my home, building harmony and stability as the foundation for my growth.

Aquarius
09 September 2026

Ambition surges as your career zone activates. Aquarius, this is an excellent day to step forward with confidence and allow your originality to shine. Recognition for past efforts may arrive, or a new responsibility could place you in a leadership role. Authority figures might test your resolve, but steady diplomacy will win the day. Don't seek approval—focus on aligning with your true vision. Strategic, consistent action will bring long-term rewards. Trust that your contributions are valued and necessary.

Affirmation & Gratitude

I step into leadership with confidence, knowing my originality creates lasting success.

Aquarius
10 September 2026

Curiosity fuels your spirit today. Aquarius, Uranus encourages you to break routine and embrace new ideas or experiences. This might mean trying a new class, traveling somewhere unfamiliar, or simply shifting your perspective through conversation. Restlessness is a signal that growth is calling. Don't dismiss unusual opportunities—they may open doors you hadn't considered. Inspiration strikes when you allow yourself to be curious and free from rigid expectations. The cosmos invites you to welcome change as an ally.

Affirmation & Gratitude
I embrace curiosity and change, trusting new experiences to expand my wisdom and joy.

Aquarius
11 September 2026

Relationships come into focus. Venus emphasizes balance, love, and connection, but she also highlights areas where harmony may be lacking. If you've been giving too much, or withholding your needs, today is about restoring equality. Healthy partnerships support individuality while encouraging closeness. Whether romantic, platonic, or professional, this is a day to nurture connections that uplift you. Be honest, but also gentle—authentic communication strengthens bonds.

Affirmation & Gratitude
I welcome balanced connections, embracing honesty, love, and respect in all relationships.

Aquarius
12 September 2026

Introspection is emphasized under today's cosmic energy. Aquarius, you may feel more sensitive than usual, but this is an invitation to pause and go within. Old emotions or unresolved memories may resurface, showing you what still needs release. Solitude, journaling, or meditation will provide clarity. Don't push for outward productivity—inner renewal is the true accomplishment today. Trust that stillness is not wasted time but a gift that restores your strength for the next phase.

Affirmation & Gratitude

I honor stillness and reflection, trusting my inner wisdom to renew clarity and peace.

Aquarius
13 September 2026

The Moon in your sign amplifies your presence and energy, Aquarius. You feel magnetic, expressive, and ready to step into visibility. This is an excellent time to set intentions, begin new projects, or simply embrace your individuality unapologetically. Others are drawn to your authenticity, and opportunities may present themselves when you share your truth with confidence. Be patient with yourself—progress takes time, but every step you take today plants meaningful seeds.

Affirmation & Gratitude

I shine authentically, embracing my individuality with confidence and joy.

Aquarius
14 September 2026

Finances and values come under review. Aquarius, the cosmos urges you to consider whether your spending habits, investments, and use of energy align with your long-term goals. Emotional triggers around money may surface, but see them as guidance toward wiser decisions. True abundance is about balance—time, energy, health, and peace are as valuable as money. Today is about choosing stability and freedom over short-term gratification. Align your daily actions with your higher vision.

Affirmation & Gratitude

I align my resources with wisdom, creating stability that sustains freedom and peace.

Aquarius
15 September 2026

Communication is emphasized today, Aquarius. Mercury boosts your ability to share ideas clearly and persuasively, making this an excellent day for writing, presenting, or teaching. Inspiration may come through an unexpected conversation or message, so keep an open mind. Your originality makes your words impactful, but don't overwhelm others with too much detail—clarity and focus will be most effective. Balance speaking with active listening, as wisdom can flow both ways. Use today to exchange knowledge, knowing your words can plant seeds of lasting impact.

Affirmation & Gratitude

I express myself with clarity and authenticity, trusting my words to inspire connection and growth.

Aquarius
16 September 2026

Emotional matters tied to home and family rise to the surface. Aquarius, you may feel pulled to address household responsibilities, nurture loved ones, or simply create balance in your personal space. If conflicts arise, meet them with patience and compassion, not defensiveness. Your home is a reflection of your inner world, and when harmony exists there, your energy flows more freely into other areas of life. Today favors grounding yourself, creating peace, and tending to emotional security.

Affirmation & Gratitude

I create harmony at home, nurturing peace and stability as the roots of my growth.

Aquarius
17 September 2026

Career ambitions are spotlighted today. Aquarius, opportunities may arise to demonstrate your leadership or innovative thinking. Recognition could come, but it requires you to step forward confidently. Challenges with authority figures are possible—handle them with calm diplomacy. Stay true to your vision, even if others don't fully understand it yet. Progress today is not about rushing ahead but about building credibility through steady, consistent effort. Plant seeds now, and they will blossom into future success.

Affirmation & Gratitude

I step into leadership with confidence, trusting my originality to guide long-term success.

Aquarius
18 September 2026

Curiosity and exploration call, Aquarius. Uranus stirs your adventurous side, making today ideal for learning, travel, or breaking routine. Inspiration may arrive unexpectedly through a conversation, new knowledge, or an encounter with someone who expands your perspective. Growth often comes when you say yes to unfamiliar paths. Don't resist change—embrace it as a doorway to freedom. Today is about allowing your spirit to wander and your mind to stretch beyond limits.

Affirmation & Gratitude

I embrace new experiences with curiosity, trusting change to expand my wisdom and joy.

Aquarius
19 September 2026

Relationships are in focus. Aquarius, Venus emphasizes harmony but also reveals imbalances in how you give and receive. This is an opportunity to restore equality through open, kind conversations. Romantic energy feels vibrant, and professional collaborations thrive under mutual respect. Choose partnerships that celebrate individuality while encouraging closeness. If single, you may feel drawn to someone who resonates with your unique energy. The universe reminds you that love should uplift, never restrict.

Affirmation & Gratitude

I welcome balanced partnerships, honoring love, freedom, and respect in all my connections.

Aquarius
20 September 2026

Introspection and healing are emphasized. Aquarius, today encourages you to pause, reflect, and process emotions that may resurface. Solitude can bring clarity, especially through journaling, meditation, or quiet time in nature. Old patterns may reappear, but they're here to be acknowledged and released. Don't view rest as wasted time—it's essential for renewal. By listening inwardly, you'll find the insight and strength you need to move forward with clarity.

Affirmation & Gratitude

I honor stillness and reflection, trusting my inner wisdom to restore peace and clarity.

Aquarius
21 September 2026

The Moon in your sign energizes you with vitality and presence. Aquarius, today is excellent for stepping into the spotlight, expressing yourself, or beginning projects that require courage. Your authenticity draws others toward you, and opportunities flow when you shine unapologetically. Progress may feel exciting but remember to pace yourself. Step-by-step action ensures lasting growth. The cosmos reminds you that your individuality is not only your gift—it's your greatest strength.

Affirmation & Gratitude

I shine authentically, embracing my individuality with confidence and joy.

Aquarius
22 September 2026

Finances and resources take priority today. Aquarius, the cosmos urges you to check whether your current spending, saving, and use of time are aligned with your long-term vision. Emotional spending may tempt you, but discipline brings greater peace. Abundance is more than possessions—it's also about energy, health, and freedom. Today is an opportunity to realign your daily choices with your higher values. Even small adjustments can shift you toward greater security and stability.

Affirmation & Gratitude

I manage my resources wisely, creating stability that supports my freedom and peace of mind.

Aquarius
23 September 2026

Communication is energized today. Aquarius, Mercury enhances your ability to express ideas with clarity, making this an excellent time for teaching, presenting, or networking. Inspiration may come through a conversation, so pay attention to synchronicities. Be mindful not to scatter your energy—direct your focus toward one or two meaningful priorities. Your originality gives your words weight, and people are listening. Use this opportunity to plant seeds through authentic dialogue.

Affirmation & Gratitude

I communicate with clarity and authenticity, trusting my words to inspire and connect.

Aquarius
24 September 2026

Emotional matters tied to home and family may come to the forefront. Aquarius, you may feel called to nurture your sanctuary, whether through connecting with loved ones, improving your living space, or addressing sensitive issues. Handle tensions with patience and compassion rather than defensiveness. Creating peace at home strengthens your foundation, giving you more stability to pursue goals elsewhere. The cosmos reminds you that harmony within creates harmony without.

Affirmation & Gratitude

I create peace in my home, nurturing stability and balance at my roots.

Aquarius
25 September 2026

Ambition rises as your career zone lights up. Aquarius, opportunities for recognition or advancement may arrive, but they require you to step forward with confidence. Authority figures may test you—respond with diplomacy and clarity. Today is about proving your persistence and vision rather than seeking instant validation. By staying consistent, your originality will be noticed. This is a day to take practical steps toward your bigger professional goals.

Affirmation & Gratitude

I step confidently toward success, trusting my originality to guide me forward.

Aquarius
26 September 2026

Curiosity fuels your spirit. Aquarius, Uranus stirs a desire for variety and growth, making this a perfect day to try something new. Whether through study, exploration, or conversation, inspiration will arrive when you step outside your comfort zone. Unexpected encounters may shift your perspective. Don't fear change—embrace it as a tool for growth. This is a day for fresh insights, so follow where curiosity leads you.

Affirmation & Gratitude

I embrace curiosity and change, trusting new experiences to expand my wisdom.

Aquarius
27 September 2026

Relationships are emphasized today. Aquarius, Venus encourages harmony but also shines a light on imbalances. If you've been overextending or holding back, today is about restoring equality. Authentic partnerships support individuality as much as closeness. Romantic connections feel nurturing, while professional collaborations may strengthen through fairness. Remember, the relationships that matter most will always celebrate your uniqueness.

Affirmation & Gratitude

I welcome balanced, authentic relationships that honor love, respect, and freedom.

Aquarius
28 September 2026

Introspection is favored. Aquarius, today invites you to slow down and reconnect with your inner self. Old emotions or patterns may surface, but they're ready to be acknowledged and released. This is a day for journaling, meditation, or quiet reflection. Don't push yourself to be overly productive —rest and renewal are your greatest achievements now. Trust that clarity comes when you listen inwardly.

Affirmation & Gratitude

I honor rest and reflection, trusting inner stillness to restore peace and clarity.

Aquarius
29 September 2026

The Moon in your sign amplifies your vitality, Aquarius. You feel magnetic, expressive, and more comfortable stepping into visibility. Use this energy to launch a new project, express your ideas, or simply embrace your uniqueness more boldly. People are drawn to your authenticity, and opportunities may arise when you own your individuality unapologetically. Progress may feel exciting but remember to pace yourself —lasting growth is steady.

Affirmation & Gratitude

I shine authentically, embracing my individuality with courage and joy.

Aquarius
30 September 2026

September closes with a call for review and gratitude. Aquarius, reflect on the lessons of the past month. Where have you embraced growth, balance, or originality? Where do adjustments still need to be made? Celebrate your achievements, even small ones, and honor the progress you've made. Journaling, meditation, or a gratitude ritual will help you integrate your experiences and step into October with clarity and strength. The cosmos reminds you that reflection fuels alignment.

Affirmation & Gratitude

I reflect with gratitude, honoring my growth and preparing for October with clarity.

October 2026

Aquarius
01 October 2026

October begins with a strong focus on shared resources and trust, Aquarius. The cosmos encourages you to reflect on how you handle give-and-take in your life—whether with money, time, or emotional investment. Transparency will be key, especially if conversations about joint finances or partnerships surface. Avoid power struggles by choosing openness and honesty. This is also a day to consider whether you're holding back out of fear. The universe is asking you to let go of control and trust in balance. Transformation often begins with vulnerability.

Affirmation & Gratitude

I embrace honesty and trust, allowing balance in shared energy to create deeper connections.

Aquarius
02 October 2026

Your sense of adventure is awakened today. Aquarius, Uranus stirs curiosity and a desire for expansion, making this an excellent time for travel, study, or exploring a new perspective. You may encounter someone whose ideas challenge you, inspiring growth. Restlessness may push you to break routine —follow it, but in constructive ways. The universe reminds you that life thrives when you're willing to embrace change. Inspiration and freedom arrive when you say yes to exploration.

Affirmation & Gratitude

I welcome new experiences with curiosity, trusting change to guide my growth and wisdom.

Aquarius
03 October 2026

Relationships are in focus. Venus highlights connection, love, and collaboration. Aquarius, this is a day to strengthen bonds by practicing equality and open communication. If imbalance exists, you'll feel it strongly now, urging you to restore harmony. Romantic connections feel warm, while professional or social partnerships thrive under fairness and respect. Don't compromise your individuality for peace—true connection uplifts both sides. The cosmos reminds you that love rooted in authenticity always endures.

Affirmation & Gratitude

I cultivate balanced relationships, honoring freedom, love, and respect in all connections.

Aquarius
04 October 2026

Reflection and solitude are emphasized. Aquarius, the cosmos draws you inward, encouraging rest and introspection. Old emotions may resurface, showing you where healing is needed. This is not a day to push yourself toward productivity, but to honor stillness. Meditation, journaling, or quiet walks in nature can provide clarity. Your intuition is strong now—listen closely. The universe reminds you that growth often happens in silence, when you allow space for insight to arise.

Affirmation & Gratitude

I honor stillness and reflection, trusting my inner wisdom to restore clarity and strength.

Aquarius
05 October 2026

The Moon in your sign brings a surge of energy and confidence. Aquarius, today you feel magnetic, and your individuality shines. This is the perfect time to start a project, share your ideas, or embrace your uniqueness unapologetically. Others are drawn to your authenticity, and opportunities may appear when you confidently stand in your truth. Be mindful of impatience—progress grows step by step. The cosmos supports you in stepping boldly into visibility.

Affirmation & Gratitude

I shine authentically, embracing my individuality with confidence and joy.

Aquarius
06 October 2026

Finances and values are highlighted today. Aquarius, review how your resources—money, time, and energy—are being used. Emotional spending could tempt you, but discipline will serve you better. True abundance is not only material—it's also the balance of health, time, and peace of mind. Small steps you take now to align your spending and energy with your long-term goals will bring security and freedom. Today is about making wise, grounded choices.

Affirmation & Gratitude

I align my resources with my values, creating stability that sustains freedom and peace.

Aquarius
07 October 2026

Communication flows effortlessly today. Aquarius, Mercury sharpens your mind and voice, making this a powerful day for writing, teaching, or having important discussions. Inspiration may come through an unexpected conversation—stay alert. Don't scatter your energy across too many tasks. Focus on sharing your message clearly and authentically. Listening is just as valuable as speaking, and wisdom may come through others' perspectives. The universe is encouraging you to embrace dialogue as a tool for growth.

Affirmation & Gratitude

I communicate with clarity and confidence, trusting my words to inspire and connect.

Aquarius
08 October 2026

Emotional matters around home and family come into focus. Aquarius, you may feel the need to nurture your private life, whether by improving your living space, resolving family dynamics, or reconnecting with loved ones. If tensions surface, approach them gently—healing flows more easily when compassion leads the way. Your home is more than walls and rooms; it's the energy that supports your spirit. Creating harmony there today will ground you for the bigger ambitions ahead.

Affirmation & Gratitude

I nurture harmony in my home, building peace and stability as the foundation of my dreams.

Aquarius
09 October 2026

Ambition rises as your career sector activates. Aquarius, you may find yourself stepping into leadership or being recognized for your originality. Don't shy away from responsibility; you have what it takes to succeed. Authority figures may test your patience, but calm persistence will earn respect. This is a day for action and strategy, not shortcuts. Take one step toward your professional goals today, knowing consistency now sets you up for long-term success.

Affirmation & Gratitude

I step into leadership with confidence, trusting my originality to guide lasting achievement.

Aquarius
10 October 2026

Curiosity leads the way today. Aquarius, Uranus stirs your adventurous side, encouraging you to explore outside your comfort zone. Whether through travel, study, or simply meeting new people, you'll find inspiration in variety. Restlessness is a sign you're ready for change—don't resist it. An unexpected encounter may shift your outlook in profound ways. The universe reminds you that fresh perspectives often bring breakthroughs, so follow your curiosity.

Affirmation & Gratitude

I embrace new experiences with curiosity, trusting change to expand my wisdom and joy.

Aquarius
11 October 2026

Relationships are emphasized. Aquarius, Venus highlights harmony, but she also brings attention to any imbalance you've been ignoring. This is your opportunity to restore equality by being honest with yourself and others. Romantic sparks may feel stronger now, and professional collaborations thrive when fairness leads the way. Healthy partnerships uplift and respect your individuality rather than confine it. Choose connections that allow you to flourish as your authentic self.

Affirmation & Gratitude
I welcome balanced, authentic relationships that honor freedom, love, and respect.

Aquarius
12 October 2026

Introspection takes center stage. Aquarius, today is not for pushing ahead but for listening inward. Old emotions may resurface—acknowledge them without judgment. Solitude, journaling, or meditation can bring clarity and healing. Rest is productive when it allows you to realign with your true path. Trust your intuition and pay attention to subtle signs—they may hold the answers you've been seeking. Stillness is a gift today; use it wisely.

Affirmation & Gratitude

I honor reflection, trusting inner wisdom to bring clarity, healing, and renewal.

Aquarius
13 October 2026

The Moon in your sign revitalizes you, Aquarius. Today you feel magnetic, expressive, and eager to stand in your truth. This is a powerful day for setting intentions, beginning projects, or embracing your individuality more boldly. People notice your authenticity, and opportunities may appear as a result of your confidence. Be mindful not to rush—progress grows stronger with patience. Shine unapologetically, and trust that your uniqueness is your strength.

Affirmation & Gratitude

I shine authentically, embracing my individuality as a source of strength and inspiration.

Aquarius
14 October 2026

Finances and resources demand attention. Aquarius, review your relationship with abundance today. Are your habits supporting your long-term goals or undermining them? Emotional spending may tempt you, but discipline will serve you better. Abundance is not only about money—it's about aligning your energy, time, and resources with what truly matters. Make small, practical adjustments now to build long-term security. Today is about valuing yourself enough to make wise, empowering choices.

Affirmation & Gratitude

I align my choices with my values, creating stability that sustains freedom and peace.

Aquarius
15 October 2026

Communication flows with ease today, Aquarius. Mercury sharpens your wit and clarity, making this an excellent time for teaching, writing, or meaningful discussions. A casual conversation may hold surprising insight, so stay open. Your originality shines through your words, but remember that simplicity often carries the most impact. Listening is just as important as speaking—wisdom is exchanged in both directions. Today is about building bridges through honest dialogue and letting your voice inspire others.

Affirmation & Gratitude

I communicate with clarity and openness, trusting my words to inspire connection and growth.

Aquarius
16 October 2026

Family and home life call for attention. Aquarius, the cosmos encourages you to ground yourself in your private world. You may feel pulled to create harmony in your environment or address emotional dynamics within family relationships. If tensions arise, patience and compassion will be key. Remember, your home is the foundation that supports your bigger ambitions. By bringing balance to your sanctuary, you create a strong base from which to thrive outwardly.

Affirmation & Gratitude
I nurture harmony in my home, building stability and peace at my roots.

Aquarius
17 October 2026

Ambition rises as your career zone lights up. Aquarius, today's energy may place you in the spotlight, offering recognition for your efforts or a chance to step into leadership. Authority figures may test you, but diplomacy will carry more weight than confrontation. Stay true to your vision and trust that persistence wins over quick wins. Every action you take today builds credibility, setting the stage for future success. Your originality is your greatest strength—let it shine.

Affirmation & Gratitude

I step into leadership with confidence, building success through persistence and authenticity.

Aquarius
18 October 2026

Curiosity and adventure drive you forward today. Aquarius, Uranus inspires you to explore beyond your comfort zone. Whether through study, travel, or connecting with someone who offers a fresh perspective, growth is available if you embrace it. Don't dismiss unusual opportunities—they may hold the breakthroughs you've been waiting for. Restlessness is a signal from the cosmos that it's time to expand. Change isn't chaos—it's the path to freedom.

Affirmation & Gratitude

I embrace curiosity and change, trusting exploration to expand my wisdom and joy.

Aquarius
19 October 2026

Relationships take center stage. Aquarius, Venus highlights harmony but also brings your awareness to any imbalances you may be tolerating. This is the perfect day to address equality in your partnerships with honesty and compassion. Romantic bonds feel especially warm, and professional collaborations may deepen if rooted in fairness. Remember, healthy connections support individuality while fostering closeness. Choose the relationships that uplift and celebrate who you truly are.

Affirmation & Gratitude

I cultivate balanced, authentic connections that honor love, respect, and individuality.

Aquarius
20 October 2026

Reflection is encouraged today. Aquarius, you may feel more sensitive and introspective, making this a good time for journaling, meditation, or simply taking space for yourself. Old emotions may arise, but they are guiding you toward release and healing. Don't pressure yourself to achieve outwardly—inner clarity is the real accomplishment now. Trust your intuition; the whispers of your soul carry guidance. By slowing down, you align yourself with what truly matters.

Affirmation & Gratitude

I honor stillness and reflection, trusting my inner wisdom to guide my growth.

Aquarius
21 October 2026

The Moon in your sign energizes you with vitality and presence. Aquarius, today you feel magnetic, expressive, and ready to embrace visibility. This is a wonderful time to begin projects, set intentions, or simply express yourself without hesitation. Others are drawn to your authenticity, and opportunities may arise when you step forward confidently. Be patient with progress—it builds step by step. The cosmos is reminding you that your individuality is your superpower.

Affirmation & Gratitude
I shine authentically, embracing my individuality as my greatest strength.

Aquarius
22 October 2026

Finances and values come into sharp focus. Aquarius, the cosmos is asking you to look closely at how you manage money, time, and energy. Emotional triggers may surface around spending, but they are clues to deeper patterns. True abundance isn't about possessions—it's about aligning resources with your highest goals. Reflect on whether your current choices create stability or drain your freedom. Even small adjustments today can have powerful long-term results. Take practical steps and trust yourself to build security.

Affirmation & Gratitude

I align my resources with my values, creating stability that nurtures freedom and peace.

Aquarius
23 October 2026

Communication is heightened today. Aquarius, Mercury boosts your ability to speak clearly and persuasively, making this a wonderful time for writing, teaching, or sharing your ideas. A casual conversation may bring inspiration or open an unexpected door. Don't scatter your attention—focus your words where they matter most. Your originality is magnetic now, so let your authentic voice lead. Balance speaking with listening; insight flows both ways when dialogue is genuine.

Affirmation & Gratitude
I communicate with clarity and confidence, trusting my words to inspire and connect.

Aquarius
24 October 2026

Emotional matters tied to home or family rise to the surface. Aquarius, today is about nurturing your roots and ensuring your sanctuary feels balanced. You may feel the urge to reorganize your space, reconnect with loved ones, or resolve old tensions. Approach discussions with compassion rather than defensiveness. Your home is the anchor that supports your bigger dreams—create peace here and you'll feel stronger everywhere else. Ground yourself through acts of care and connection.

Affirmation & Gratitude
I nurture harmony within my home, creating peace and stability at my foundation.

Aquarius
25 October 2026

Ambition and recognition are highlighted. Aquarius, your career sector is active, and opportunities may arise to step forward into leadership. You could receive acknowledgment for past efforts, or a new responsibility could push you to showcase your originality. Authority figures may test your patience, but diplomacy is key. Success comes through consistent, steady action rather than shortcuts. Trust that your uniqueness is exactly what's needed now. Don't dim your light—let it lead.

Affirmation & Gratitude

I step into leadership with confidence, trusting my originality to guide lasting success.

Aquarius
26 October 2026

Curiosity fuels your spirit today. Aquarius, Uranus inspires you to expand your worldview, whether through study, travel, or meaningful conversations. Restlessness is a sign that growth is calling. Don't dismiss unusual opportunities—they may provide the breakthrough you've been waiting for. Inspiration strikes when you leave your comfort zone, so follow your curiosity with confidence. Change isn't disruption—it's transformation. Today, the universe encourages you to see the unfamiliar as a gift.

Affirmation & Gratitude

I embrace new experiences with curiosity, trusting change to expand my wisdom and joy.

Aquarius
27 October 2026

Relationships are in focus. Aquarius, Venus encourages harmony, but she also highlights imbalance if you've been avoiding it. Are you giving more than you receive, or withholding too much? Today invites you to restore equality through honesty and kindness. Romantic energy feels supportive, while professional partnerships may grow stronger if rooted in respect. Remember, authentic love and collaboration celebrate individuality rather than diminish it. Choose bonds that let you be fully yourself.

Affirmation & Gratitude

I cultivate balanced, authentic relationships that honor love, respect, and freedom.

Aquarius
28 October 2026

Reflection is encouraged. Aquarius, the cosmos draws your energy inward, asking you to pause and honor your inner world. Old emotions may surface, offering a chance for release and healing. This is not a day for forcing outcomes but for listening to your intuition. Solitude, journaling, or meditation will provide clarity. Trust that rest is not wasted—it is the foundation of your next step. By slowing down, you align more deeply with your true self.

Affirmation & Gratitude

I honor stillness and reflection, trusting inner wisdom to bring peace and renewal.

Aquarius
29 October 2026

The Moon in your sign recharges you, Aquarius. Today you feel magnetic, energized, and eager to express your individuality. This is the perfect time to start a project, set bold intentions, or step into visibility. Others are drawn to your authenticity, and opportunities may follow when you share your truth unapologetically. Be patient with your progress—it builds steadily with consistency. The cosmos is reminding you to embrace your uniqueness as your greatest strength.

Affirmation & Gratitude

I shine authentically, embracing my individuality as my source of strength and joy.

Aquarius
30 October 2026

Finances and values take the spotlight. Aquarius, today invites you to review whether your resources are aligned with your higher vision. Money may be a theme, but so too are time and energy. Emotional spending may tempt you, but the cosmos urges discipline. Abundance comes when you choose wisely and honor your worth. Small, practical steps taken now build long-term stability and freedom. Remember: true wealth is balance, not excess.

Affirmation & Gratitude

I align my resources with wisdom, creating abundance that sustains freedom and peace.

Aquarius
31 October 2026

October ends with a reflective yet empowering tone. Aquarius, the cosmos asks you to review your progress this month. Where have you embraced authenticity, balance, or growth? What lessons are worth carrying forward, and what can you release? Today is ideal for journaling, meditation, or gratitude practice. Celebrate your wins, no matter how small, and honor the shifts you've made. The universe reminds you that acknowledging your journey strengthens your spirit for the road ahead.

Affirmation & Gratitude

I reflect with gratitude, honoring my growth and preparing for November with clarity and strength.

November 2026

Aquarius
01 November 2026

November opens with energy centered on shared resources, trust, and deeper emotional truths. Aquarius, you may find yourself drawn into conversations about money, joint ventures, or partnerships. Transparency will be essential—hidden details could surface. This is also a time to reflect on how much you give and receive in relationships. Are the scales balanced, or are adjustments needed? Vulnerability may feel uncomfortable, but leaning into honesty strengthens bonds. The cosmos invites you to clear what no longer serves, so you can step into this month empowered.

Affirmation & Gratitude

I embrace honesty and balance, trusting transparency to deepen trust and connection.

Aquarius
02 November 2026

Adventure calls, Aquarius. Uranus awakens your curiosity, making this a perfect day for exploring beyond the ordinary. This could manifest through travel, new studies, or fresh experiences that shake up your usual rhythm. Encounters with people from different backgrounds may inspire new ways of thinking. Don't dismiss unusual opportunities—they may carry the seeds of transformation. Restlessness today is a sign that growth is waiting for you. The universe encourages you to say yes to the unknown.

Affirmation & Gratitude

I welcome change and exploration, trusting curiosity to guide me toward growth.

Aquarius
03 November 2026

Relationships are highlighted. Venus emphasizes harmony but also draws your attention to where balance may be off. Aquarius, it's a good day to strengthen bonds by speaking openly and kindly about your needs. Authenticity is essential—don't compromise who you are just to keep the peace. Romantic connections feel especially warm, and professional partnerships can deepen if mutual respect is present. The cosmos reminds you that healthy love and collaboration honor individuality as much as togetherness.

Affirmation & Gratitude

I cultivate relationships that honor equality, love, and authenticity.

Aquarius
04 November 2026

Introspection is favored. Aquarius, the cosmos encourages you to slow down, rest, and listen to your inner voice. Old memories or emotions may resurface, asking for release. Don't resist—healing comes when you allow yourself to acknowledge and let go. Journaling, meditation, or creative solitude can provide valuable clarity. Productivity is not measured in tasks completed today but in the insights you gain. Trust your intuition—it carries important guidance for your next steps.

Affirmation & Gratitude

I honor stillness and reflection, trusting my intuition to restore clarity and peace.

Aquarius
05 November 2026

The Moon in your sign recharges your energy, Aquarius. You feel magnetic and ready to express your individuality more boldly. This is an excellent day to set intentions, begin projects, or share your ideas with others. Your authenticity attracts opportunities, and people notice when you step forward with confidence. Be mindful of impatience—progress takes time. The cosmos encourages you to shine brightly today and trust that your uniqueness is your superpower.

Affirmation & Gratitude

I shine authentically, embracing my individuality with courage and joy.

Aquarius
06 November 2026

Finances and values are highlighted. Aquarius, review your relationship with abundance. Are your spending and saving habits aligned with your bigger vision? Emotional triggers around money may surface, but they offer insight. True wealth is more than material—it's also time, health, and peace of mind. Small, practical choices today will build long-term freedom and stability. The universe asks you to value yourself enough to direct resources wisely.

Affirmation & Gratitude

I make wise choices with my resources, creating abundance that supports freedom and peace.

Aquarius
07 November 2026

Communication flows easily today. Aquarius, Mercury enhances your ability to express ideas clearly and persuasively. This is an excellent day for writing, teaching, or engaging in important conversations. Inspiration may strike through an unexpected message or encounter, so stay receptive. Balance speaking with listening—dialogue today can spark insights that shift your path forward. Authenticity ensures your words resonate deeply. The cosmos encourages you to share your truth without hesitation.

Affirmation & Gratitude

I express myself with clarity and openness, trusting my words to inspire and connect.

Aquarius
08 November 2026

Home and family matters rise to the surface today. Aquarius, the cosmos calls for you to focus on your private world, strengthening your foundation and creating harmony in your living space. If family dynamics feel unsettled, address them with patience and compassion rather than defensiveness. Your sanctuary is a reflection of your inner state—tend to it, and you'll feel more balanced in all areas of life. Even simple gestures, like cleaning or reorganizing, can have powerful effects on your spirit.

Affirmation & Gratitude

I nurture harmony within my home, creating peace and stability at my foundation.

Aquarius
09 November 2026

Ambition comes into play as your career zone activates. Aquarius, opportunities may arise for recognition or for you to step into leadership. Your originality is your greatest asset, so let it shine. Authority figures may test your patience, but calm diplomacy will help you earn respect. This is a day to take steady steps toward your goals rather than rushing. Remember, consistent effort builds the reputation and foundation needed for long-term success.

Affirmation & Gratitude

I step into leadership with confidence, trusting my originality to create lasting success.

Aquarius
10 November 2026

Curiosity fuels your spirit. Aquarius, Uranus inspires you to explore beyond the familiar. This could be through study, travel, or new conversations that expand your worldview. Restlessness may stir, but it's a signal that growth is waiting. Unexpected encounters could bring inspiration or ideas that shift your path forward. Don't fear the unknown —embrace it as an ally. Today the universe invites you to broaden your perspective and welcome change as a tool for growth.

Affirmation & Gratitude

I embrace curiosity and change, trusting new experiences to expand my wisdom.

Aquarius
11 November 2026

Relationships are emphasized. Aquarius, Venus brings harmony but also shows where imbalance may exist. If you've been giving more than you receive—or holding back—this is your opportunity to restore balance. Romantic energy is supportive, while professional collaborations may thrive with fairness and mutual respect. Authentic love and partnership never ask you to shrink; they encourage you to flourish. Choose connections that uplift your individuality and allow you to be fully yourself.

Affirmation & Gratitude

I welcome balanced relationships that honor love, respect, and freedom.

Aquarius
12 November 2026

Reflection and introspection are encouraged today. Aquarius, the cosmos asks you to pause, rest, and tune into your inner world. Old emotions or memories may resurface, but they carry wisdom if you're willing to listen. Stillness allows you to release what no longer serves. This is not a day for overexertion but for gentle self-care. Journaling, meditation, or simply quiet time in nature will help you regain clarity and strength.

Affirmation & Gratitude

I honor stillness and reflection, trusting my inner wisdom to guide me with clarity.

Aquarius
13 November 2026

The Moon in your sign recharges your vitality and confidence, Aquarius. Today you feel magnetic, expressive, and ready to step into visibility. This is a wonderful time to start fresh projects, embrace new opportunities, or simply assert your individuality with pride. Others are drawn to your authenticity, and doors may open when you boldly share your truth. Be careful not to rush into everything at once—pace yourself so you can sustain progress. The universe is encouraging you to own your uniqueness and let it shine without apology.

Affirmation & Gratitude

I shine authentically, embracing my individuality as my greatest strength and gift to the world.

Aquarius
14 November 2026

Finances and values are emphasized today. Aquarius, the cosmos encourages you to reflect on whether your current habits are aligned with your long-term vision. Emotional triggers around money may arise, but they are invitations to make wiser choices. True wealth is not just financial—it's also peace of mind, health, and energy. Focus on small, practical adjustments that bring stability and freedom. By aligning your resources with your higher values, you ensure lasting security. Today is about honoring your worth through smart, intentional choices.

Affirmation & Gratitude

I align my resources with wisdom, creating abundance that sustains freedom and peace.

Aquarius
15 November 2026

Communication is spotlighted today, Aquarius. Mercury enhances your ability to express yourself with clarity and originality. This is an excellent day for writing, teaching, or having meaningful discussions. A casual conversation could spark inspiration or open a door you didn't expect, so stay open to synchronicities. Focus your energy rather than scattering it—your words are powerful and will carry influence. Balance speaking with active listening, as wisdom can flow both ways. The universe encourages you to use dialogue as a tool for connection and growth.

Affirmation & Gratitude

I communicate with clarity and openness, trusting my words to inspire meaningful change.

Aquarius
16 November 2026

Emotional matters tied to home or family may surface today. Aquarius, you may feel called to nurture your sanctuary, address household responsibilities, or resolve tensions with loved ones. Your home is more than just a physical space—it's an energetic foundation that supports you. If emotions run high, meet them with patience and compassion. Reorganizing or beautifying your living environment can also restore peace. By grounding yourself today, you create the stability needed for your greater ambitions to thrive.

Affirmation & Gratitude

I create harmony in my home, nurturing peace and stability at my foundation.

Aquarius
17 November 2026

Career and ambition take focus. Aquarius, opportunities may arise that push you into the spotlight or call on you to lead. Recognition is possible, but it will require persistence and strategy. Challenges with authority figures might test your resolve, yet diplomacy will carry more weight than confrontation. This is not a day for shortcuts—steady, consistent action builds credibility. Trust that your originality is a strength, and step into your role with confidence.

Affirmation & Gratitude

I step into leadership with confidence, trusting my originality to guide lasting success.

Aquarius
18 November 2026

Curiosity and exploration are calling. Aquarius, Uranus stirs a restlessness that invites you to try new things and break away from stale patterns. This might mean exploring a new subject, traveling, or engaging in conversations that stretch your worldview. Growth today comes from saying yes to what feels unfamiliar. Don't let fear of change hold you back—embrace the unknown as an ally. Fresh insights and breakthroughs are waiting for you outside your comfort zone.

Affirmation & Gratitude

I embrace curiosity and welcome change, trusting new experiences to expand my wisdom and spirit.

Aquarius
19 November 2026

Relationships are highlighted under today's cosmic influence. Aquarius, Venus encourages warmth, harmony, and closeness, but also reveals imbalances that may need attention. If you've been giving more than you're receiving—or holding back your needs—this is a chance to restore balance. Healthy connections respect individuality while allowing space for intimacy. Romantic bonds feel supportive now, while professional collaborations thrive under fairness and mutual respect. Choose the relationships that uplift you and honor your truth.

Affirmation & Gratitude

I welcome balanced relationships, embracing love, respect, and authenticity in all connections.

Aquarius
20 November 2026

Introspection is emphasized today. Aquarius, the cosmos invites you to slow down and reconnect with your inner world. Old emotions or unresolved issues may resurface, but they are showing you where healing is needed. Take time for journaling, meditation, or rest. Don't pressure yourself to produce outwardly—progress today is measured in clarity gained. The universe reminds you that wisdom often arises when you allow silence and stillness to lead the way.

Affirmation & Gratitude
I honor reflection and stillness, trusting my inner wisdom to bring clarity and peace.

Aquarius
21 November 2026

The Moon in your sign energizes you with vitality and confidence. Aquarius, today you feel magnetic and ready to shine. This is an excellent day to set bold intentions, embrace new opportunities, or simply live more authentically. Others are drawn to your individuality, and opportunities may arise when you step forward courageously. Be mindful of impatience—growth takes time. The cosmos reminds you that your uniqueness is your greatest strength.

Affirmation & Gratitude

I shine authentically, embracing my individuality as my source of confidence and joy.

Aquarius
22 November 2026

Finances and values are highlighted today. Aquarius, the cosmos invites you to examine how you manage your money, time, and energy. Emotional triggers may arise around spending or resources, but they reveal patterns that need attention. Abundance is not only financial—it also includes your peace, your health, and your time. Today is about aligning daily choices with your long-term vision. Even small adjustments can strengthen your sense of security and freedom.

Affirmation & Gratitude

I manage my resources wisely, creating abundance that supports peace and freedom in my life.

Aquarius
23 November 2026

Communication takes center stage. Aquarius, Mercury sharpens your mind and makes it easier to share your ideas with clarity and originality. This is a favorable time for writing, teaching, networking, or having important conversations. A casual dialogue may bring an unexpected breakthrough, so remain open to what others share. Remember, balance speaking with listening—wisdom comes in both directions. Your voice holds power today, so speak authentically and allow others to be inspired.

Affirmation & Gratitude

I communicate with clarity and authenticity, trusting my words to inspire growth.

Aquarius
24 November 2026

Emotional matters tied to home and family surface. Aquarius, your private world needs attention now. This may mean nurturing your physical space, resolving tensions with loved ones, or finding ways to create more comfort in your surroundings. Home is your sanctuary, and when it feels balanced, you feel more grounded in all aspects of life. Approach sensitive topics with compassion, not defensiveness. The cosmos encourages you to invest energy into peace at your roots.

Affirmation & Gratitude

I nurture harmony in my home, creating balance and stability at my foundation.

Aquarius
25 November 2026

Career ambitions come into focus. Aquarius, opportunities may present themselves that require you to step forward with courage. Recognition for your unique contributions is possible, but it may also test your patience with authority figures. Keep your cool—diplomacy ensures your vision is heard. This is a day to take practical, strategic steps toward your goals, not to chase instant success. Trust that persistence will pay off and that your originality is your greatest strength.

Affirmation & Gratitude

I step into leadership with confidence, trusting my originality to guide me forward.

Aquarius
26 November 2026

Curiosity drives you today. Aquarius, Uranus encourages you to explore beyond the usual, whether through travel, study, or conversations with people who expand your worldview. Inspiration is likely to come from unexpected sources, so be open to synchronicities. Restlessness signals your soul's need for change and growth. Don't resist the unfamiliar—it's guiding you toward new opportunities. The cosmos asks you to embrace variety as a path to wisdom and freedom.

Affirmation & Gratitude

I embrace change with curiosity, trusting new experiences to expand my wisdom.

Aquarius
27 November 2026

Relationships take center stage. Aquarius, Venus highlights harmony but also reveals imbalance where it exists. If you've been avoiding difficult conversations, today is an ideal time to approach them with compassion and honesty. Authentic love and collaboration support individuality while allowing closeness to flourish. Professional and personal partnerships can grow stronger when fairness leads. Choose connections that uplift, inspire, and allow you to be your truest self.

Affirmation & Gratitude

I cultivate balanced connections, embracing love, respect, and authenticity.

Aquarius
28 November 2026

Reflection and stillness are encouraged. Aquarius, the cosmos draws your attention inward, asking you to pause and listen to your inner voice. Old memories or emotions may resurface, but they are surfacing for release, not to weigh you down. Don't feel guilty for needing rest—healing often happens in the quieter spaces. Use today for journaling, meditation, or gentle creativity. By slowing down, you realign with your truth. The universe reminds you that wisdom often whispers when the world grows silent.

Affirmation & Gratitude

I honor stillness and reflection, trusting my inner wisdom to restore clarity and peace.

Aquarius
29 November 2026

The Moon in your sign fills you with vitality and confidence, Aquarius. Today is excellent for self-expression, new beginnings, or boldly stepping into visibility. Your originality shines brightest now, and others are naturally drawn to your authenticity. If you've been waiting to start a project or share an idea, the energy supports you. Be mindful not to rush; pace yourself so you can sustain your progress. Shine unapologetically—your individuality is your greatest strength and your most powerful magnet.

Affirmation & Gratitude

I shine authentically, embracing my individuality as my source of strength and joy.

Aquarius
30 November 2026

November closes with energy focused on values and resources. Aquarius, the cosmos asks you to review how your money, time, and energy are being invested. Are your choices building the life you truly want, or are they draining your freedom? Emotional triggers may surface, but they point you toward wiser patterns. True abundance is about more than material gain—it's about alignment between your actions and your purpose. Use today to set intentions for long-term stability.

Affirmation & Gratitude

I align my resources with wisdom, creating abundance that sustains freedom, stability, and peace.

December 2026

Aquarius
01 December 2026

December opens with your mind buzzing, Aquarius. Mercury energizes your communication zone, helping you share your ideas with clarity and originality. Conversations with friends, colleagues, or even strangers may bring unexpected breakthroughs. Networking is especially favored today—someone you meet could hold a key to future opportunities. Don't scatter your energy across too many projects; choose one or two to focus on and express yourself authentically. The cosmos reminds you that your words carry influence—use them wisely.

Affirmation & Gratitude

I share my ideas clearly and authentically, trusting my words to inspire connection and opportunity.

Aquarius
02 December 2026

Emotional matters tied to home and family surface today. Aquarius, you may feel called to strengthen your foundation by nurturing relationships or improving your living space. If tensions arise, approach them with patience and compassion. Creating harmony within your sanctuary allows you to feel more balanced in every other area of life. Simple acts—like decluttering, cooking a family meal, or spending quiet time together—can restore peace. The universe encourages you to find comfort in your roots.

Affirmation & Gratitude
I create harmony in my home, nurturing peace and stability at my foundation.

Aquarius
03 December 2026

Career ambitions take the spotlight. Aquarius, opportunities for recognition or leadership may arise today. Your originality shines, and others notice your innovative approach. Authority figures may challenge you, but diplomacy and persistence will win respect. Don't chase instant validation—focus on consistency and staying true to your vision. Seeds planted now will bear fruit in time. The cosmos encourages you to take one bold, practical step toward your long-term goals.

Affirmation & Gratitude

I step forward with confidence, trusting my originality to guide me toward lasting success.

Aquarius
04 December 2026

Curiosity and exploration are encouraged. Aquarius, Uranus inspires you to stretch beyond your comfort zone. This could be through travel, study, or simply shifting your perspective with fresh experiences. Restlessness is a signal that you're ready for growth. Pay attention to unexpected encounters—they may hold valuable insights. Don't resist change—embrace it as a tool for freedom. Today is about saying yes to opportunities that expand your spirit and sharpen your vision.

Affirmation & Gratitude

I embrace new experiences with curiosity, trusting change to expand my wisdom and freedom.

Aquarius
05 December 2026

Relationships are in focus. Aquarius, Venus emphasizes connection, harmony, and balance, but she also highlights where equality may be lacking. Are you giving too much or holding back your truth? Honest communication will restore equilibrium. Romantic sparks may feel stronger, while professional partnerships thrive when respect is mutual. Authentic connections celebrate individuality and support growth. Choose bonds that make you feel seen and valued for who you are.

Affirmation & Gratitude

I nurture balanced connections, honoring love, respect, and authenticity in all relationships.

Aquarius
06 December 2026

Reflection and stillness are emphasized. Aquarius, the cosmos draws you inward, asking you to pause and recharge. Old emotions or memories may resurface, but they are showing you what needs release. Solitude, journaling, or meditation will bring clarity and healing. Don't push yourself to produce outwardly today—inner renewal is the real work. The universe reminds you that wisdom often comes when you allow silence to guide your steps.

Affirmation & Gratitude

I honor stillness and reflection, trusting my inner wisdom to restore clarity and peace.

Aquarius
07 December 2026

The Moon in your sign fills you with energy and presence, Aquarius. Today you feel magnetic and ready to express your individuality more boldly. This is an excellent time to start projects, share your ideas, or simply enjoy being authentically yourself. Others are drawn to your originality, and opportunities may arise when you step forward with confidence. Progress may feel exciting, but remember to pace yourself. Your uniqueness is your greatest gift—share it freely.

Affirmation & Gratitude

I shine authentically, embracing my individuality with confidence and joy.

Aquarius
08 December 2026

Finances and resources are highlighted today. Aquarius, the cosmos asks you to examine how you're using your money, time, and energy. Emotional spending could tempt you, but the lesson lies in discipline. True abundance is not measured in possessions but in peace, balance, and freedom. Reflect on whether your financial habits support your bigger goals. Even small, thoughtful adjustments will create security that sustains you. Today, valuing yourself means making decisions that honor your worth and future stability.

Affirmation & Gratitude

I align my resources with wisdom, creating stability that supports freedom and peace.

Aquarius
09 December 2026

Communication flows strongly, Aquarius. Mercury enhances your clarity, making this a powerful day for teaching, writing, or having meaningful conversations. Inspiration may strike suddenly through a chance encounter or message, so stay alert. Don't dilute your truth to fit in—your originality is exactly what others need to hear. Balance your enthusiasm with attentive listening; wisdom often arrives when you allow others to speak. The cosmos encourages you to share your ideas and trust their impact.

Affirmation & Gratitude

I express myself clearly and authentically, trusting my words to inspire growth and connection.

Aquarius
10 December 2026

Family and home life come into focus today. Aquarius, the energy encourages you to tend to your private world—rearrange your living space, address unresolved tensions, or simply enjoy the comfort of being with loved ones. Your home is a mirror of your inner world; creating harmony there restores balance within yourself. If emotions run high, handle them with patience and empathy. By nurturing your foundation, you give yourself strength to pursue larger dreams.

Affirmation & Gratitude

I nurture harmony in my home, creating balance and peace at my foundation.

Aquarius
11 December 2026

Career matters rise to the surface. Aquarius, recognition or new opportunities may come your way, but they require you to step into confidence and leadership. Authority figures might test you, but diplomacy paired with originality will win respect. Today is about showing the value of your unique perspective without forcing validation. Consistent effort and authenticity will help you build a reputation that lasts. The universe supports steady progress, not shortcuts.

Affirmation & Gratitude

I step confidently toward success, trusting my originality to guide my path.

Aquarius
12 December 2026

Curiosity leads the way, Aquarius. Uranus stirs your adventurous side, making this a perfect day to seek new experiences. This could be through travel, study, or simply conversations that stretch your worldview. Restlessness signals your readiness to grow. Unexpected opportunities may present themselves—don't dismiss them. Embracing the unfamiliar can unlock breakthroughs you've been waiting for. The cosmos encourages you to see change not as disruption but as freedom in disguise.

Affirmation & Gratitude

I embrace new experiences with curiosity, trusting change to expand my wisdom and spirit.

Aquarius
13 December 2026

Relationships are emphasized under Venus's influence. Aquarius, harmony and warmth flow easily, but imbalances will also be highlighted. Have you been overextending or withholding? Today encourages honesty and openness. Romantic connections deepen with thoughtful gestures, while professional or platonic partnerships thrive under fairness and mutual respect. Remember, the best bonds celebrate individuality as much as closeness. Choose relationships that uplift and inspire rather than drain your energy.

Affirmation & Gratitude
I welcome balanced connections, embracing love, respect, and freedom in all relationships.

Aquarius
14 December 2026

Introspection is favored today. Aquarius, you may feel drawn inward to reflect, rest, and process emotions. Old patterns or memories may arise, but they're ready to be released. This is a day for journaling, meditation, or simply slowing down. Don't judge yourself for needing quiet—this pause is part of progress. The universe reminds you that stillness allows clarity to form. What you let go of today will clear the path for brighter opportunities.

Affirmation & Gratitude

I honor stillness and reflection, trusting inner wisdom to guide me toward clarity and renewal.

Aquarius
15 December 2026

The Moon in your sign energizes you, Aquarius, filling you with vitality and presence. You may feel magnetic and ready to express yourself more boldly than usual. This is an ideal day to set intentions, launch projects, or simply embrace your individuality unapologetically. Others notice your authenticity, and opportunities are more likely when you stand in your truth. Be patient—progress unfolds gradually, not all at once. The cosmos reminds you that every step counts when it's aligned with your purpose.

Affirmation & Gratitude

I shine authentically, embracing my individuality as a gift that lights my path.

Aquarius
16 December 2026

Finances and values come into sharp focus today. Aquarius, the cosmos urges you to review how your money, time, and energy are being invested. Emotional triggers may arise, but they are messages guiding you toward wiser habits. Abundance is not just material—it's also the peace you cultivate by aligning actions with your true priorities. Avoid impulsive spending; choose long-term security instead. Even small adjustments today can create ripple effects for greater freedom later.

Affirmation & Gratitude

I manage my resources with wisdom, creating stability that supports freedom and peace.

Aquarius
17 December 2026

Communication is emphasized. Aquarius, Mercury heightens your clarity and originality, making today perfect for teaching, writing, or having meaningful conversations. A chance dialogue could bring inspiration or even open new opportunities. Don't water down your truth to fit in—your voice carries unique weight when expressed authentically. Balance enthusiasm with active listening; wisdom often flows both ways. The cosmos encourages you to trust your words and use them to connect and inspire.

Affirmation & Gratitude

I communicate clearly and authentically, trusting my words to inspire growth and connection.

Aquarius
18 December 2026

Home and family matters rise to the forefront. Aquarius, the cosmos asks you to focus on your private life, whether through nurturing relationships, resolving tensions, or creating comfort in your living space. If emotions surface, meet them with patience and compassion. Your sanctuary is a reflection of your inner world—when it feels peaceful, you feel stronger everywhere else. Small, intentional efforts to bring harmony into your home will ground you deeply.

Affirmation & Gratitude

I nurture harmony within my home, creating peace and stability as my foundation.

Aquarius
19 December 2026

Career ambitions are spotlighted today. Aquarius, opportunities for recognition or responsibility may come your way. Your originality sets you apart, but remember to stay grounded and strategic. Authority figures could test you, yet responding with calm confidence will win their respect. Success today isn't about speed but about showing reliability and vision. Each step you take now plants seeds for long-term growth. The cosmos supports your persistence and encourages you to aim high.

Affirmation & Gratitude

I step confidently toward success, trusting my originality to guide lasting achievements.

Aquarius
20 December 2026

Curiosity and exploration fuel your spirit today. Aquarius, Uranus stirs restlessness, urging you to seek out new perspectives and experiences. Travel, study, or connecting with people from different walks of life can broaden your vision. Inspiration may strike in unexpected ways, so remain open. The universe reminds you that growth begins when you embrace the unfamiliar. Don't let fear hold you back—change is an ally, not a threat.

Affirmation & Gratitude

I embrace new experiences with curiosity, trusting change to expand my wisdom and freedom.

Aquarius
21 December 2026

Relationships are emphasized under Venus's influence. Aquarius, today invites harmony but also shines a light on imbalance where it exists. Romantic energy feels heightened, while professional and platonic partnerships benefit from fairness and honesty. If you've been ignoring your needs, this is the day to speak up. Authentic love and collaboration support individuality alongside closeness. Choose connections that celebrate your uniqueness and help you grow into your best self.

Affirmation & Gratitude

I welcome balanced, authentic relationships that honor love, respect, and freedom.

Aquarius
22 December 2026

Introspection is highlighted today. Aquarius, the cosmos invites you to step back, slow down, and connect with your inner self. Old emotions or memories may resurface, but they are surfacing for healing and release. Don't push yourself into productivity—today is about realignment. Solitude, meditation, or journaling will bring clarity and help you reset your energy. The universe reminds you that healing often happens in the quieter moments when you allow yourself to simply listen.

Affirmation & Gratitude
I honor stillness and reflection, trusting inner wisdom to bring me clarity and peace.

Aquarius
23 December 2026

The Moon in your sign recharges you, Aquarius, filling you with vitality and confidence. This is an excellent time to start something new, set intentions, or boldly share your vision. Your authenticity attracts attention, and others notice when you live unapologetically as yourself. Don't let impatience rush your progress—consistency is key. The cosmos supports you in stepping forward and shining in your individuality. This is a day to celebrate your uniqueness and trust in your path.

Affirmation & Gratitude
I shine authentically, embracing my individuality as my greatest strength and gift.

Aquarius
24 December 2026

Finances and resources are emphasized. Aquarius, review your spending and saving habits with honesty. Emotional triggers may arise, but they are guiding you toward wiser choices. True wealth is not only measured in money—it's also peace, freedom, and balance. Small, mindful adjustments today can strengthen your future security. By aligning your daily actions with your bigger vision, you create abundance that lasts. The cosmos encourages you to value yourself enough to make smart, intentional choices.

Affirmation & Gratitude

I manage my resources wisely, creating stability that sustains freedom and peace.

Aquarius
25 December 2026

Communication is energized. Aquarius, Mercury enhances your ability to share ideas with clarity, making this a day for heartfelt conversations and meaningful exchanges. Whether connecting with loved ones or engaging with colleagues, your words carry warmth and inspiration. Listen as much as you speak—insight flows both ways. This is also a day to express gratitude openly; your sincerity will deepen bonds. The cosmos encourages you to use your voice to uplift and inspire.

Affirmation & Gratitude

I communicate with clarity and kindness, trusting my words to create connection and joy.

Aquarius
26 December 2026

Home and family matters take priority today. Aquarius, you may feel drawn to strengthen bonds with loved ones, create comfort in your space, or resolve lingering issues. Approach situations with patience and compassion, as healing is possible now. Your sanctuary reflects your inner state, so tending to it restores balance and peace within yourself. Even small actions like cooking, decorating, or sharing quality time can shift the energy in meaningful ways.

Affirmation & Gratitude

I nurture harmony at home, creating peace and stability at my roots.

Aquarius
27 December 2026

Career ambitions are spotlighted. Aquarius, opportunities may arise for recognition or for you to step into leadership. Your originality sets you apart, but stay grounded and strategic in your approach. Authority figures may test your resolve—remain calm and diplomatic. This is a day for laying foundations rather than seeking instant rewards. Consistent effort will build credibility and pave the way for future success. The universe reminds you to trust the power of persistence.

Affirmation & Gratitude

I step confidently into success, trusting my originality to guide my path.

Aquarius
28 December 2026

Curiosity fuels you today. Aquarius, Uranus stirs a desire for exploration and growth, encouraging you to break from routine. This could come through study, travel, or simply saying yes to new experiences. Restlessness signals your readiness for expansion. Inspiration may come through unexpected encounters or conversations. The cosmos encourages you to see change not as chaos, but as opportunity. Freedom arrives when you embrace the unfamiliar.

Affirmation & Gratitude

I embrace curiosity and change, trusting new experiences to expand my wisdom and freedom.

Aquarius
29 December 2026

Relationships are in focus. Aquarius, Venus emphasizes harmony, but also highlights areas of imbalance that need your attention. Are you giving more than you receive, or holding back your needs? Today offers an opportunity to restore equality. Romantic energy feels supportive, while professional and personal partnerships strengthen under honesty and respect. Authentic love encourages individuality while fostering closeness. Choose relationships that reflect your values and allow you to grow.

Affirmation & Gratitude

I cultivate balanced, authentic connections that honor love, respect, and individuality.

Aquarius
30 December 2026

Introspection and healing are emphasized. Aquarius, the cosmos draws you inward, asking you to reflect on the past year. Old patterns or emotions may resurface, offering wisdom for the future. Take time for journaling, meditation, or gratitude practice. Don't see this pause as unproductive—it is essential for clarity. The universe is reminding you to release what no longer serves, so you can step into the new year lighter and more aligned.

Affirmation & Gratitude

I honor reflection and release, trusting stillness to prepare me for renewal.

Aquarius
31 December 2026

The year closes with powerful energy, Aquarius. The cosmos invites you to celebrate your growth while setting intentions for the year ahead. Reflect on how you've embraced your individuality, cultivated balance, and learned from challenges. This is not about perfection, but about honoring your journey. Tonight's energy favors gratitude and vision—create a ritual that helps you release the old and welcome the new. Step into 2027 with confidence, clarity, and an open heart.

Affirmation & Gratitude

I celebrate my growth and step into the new year with clarity, courage, and joy.

The Answers You Seek

Are Within

More from Amanda Clarke
The Literary Oracle
www.theliteracyoracle.com

The "Daily Guidance" series offers an innovative approach to finding spiritual wisdom and practical advice. Each book in the series is a unique tool designed for daily introspection and decision-making. Readers are invited to meditate on a question or seek general guidance for the day, then flip to a random page in the book. The page they land on provides a personalized message from various spiritual sources, such as angels, tarot, or spirit animals. With each turn of the page, these books deliver insightful, positive messages and mantras to inspire personal growth and provide clarity on life's daily challenges and decisions.

Other books in this series:-
The Angelic Oracles
Daily Angel Tarot Reading
Mystic Tarot Cat
Oracle of the Tarot Cat
Vibes Unveiled
Spirit Animal Oracle
Answers from the Oracles
Messages from the Angels

Support Indie Magic

Love your daily guidance? You can grab more of my books direct from The Literary Oracle:

www.theliteraryoracle.com

Buying direct means:
- Better prices for you
- More support for me as an indie author
- More magical books in your hands

My books are also available worldwide through online bookstores, but direct purchases help keep the magic flowing.

Thank you for supporting indie creativity!

Scan me

More on the Bookshelves at
www.theliteraryoracle.com

www.ingramcontent.com/pod-product-compliance
Lightning Source LLC
Chambersburg PA
CBHW061228070526
44584CB00030B/4033